Let's Write a Book!

A Step-by-Step Instruction Manual
for Writers

Jan-Andrew Henderson

Black Hart Entertainment

Edinburgh. Scotland

First published 2023 by Black Hart.

Black Hart Entertainment.
32 Glencoul Ave, Dalgetty Bay, Fife KY11 9XL.
6 Redgum Close, Bellbowrie QLD 4070.
blackhartentertainment.com

Copyright © 2023 by Jan-Andrew Henderson.

The rights of the author to be identified as the author of this work has been ascertained in accordance with the Copyrights, Designs and Patents Act 1988.

All rights reserved. No part of this publication may be reproduced, distributed, or transmitted in any form or by any means without prior written permission.

Book Layout © 2017 BookDesignTemplates.com
Cover by Panagiotis Lampridis (Book Design Stars).

Let's Write a Page Turner!
978-0-6454957-1-3
978-0-6454957-2-0 eBook

The definition of a page-turner really ought to be that this page is so good, you can't bear to leave it behind, but then the next page is there, and it might be just as amazing as this one.

John Burnside

I always try to tell a good story, one with a compelling plot that will keep the pages turning. That is my first and primary goal.

John Grisham

I think kids want the same thing from a book that adults want - a fast-paced story, characters worth caring about, humour, surprises, and mystery. A good book always keeps you asking questions, and makes you keep turning pages so you can find out the answers.

Rick Riordan

For Kate. Who once said long, long ago,
"You're a better writer than I expected you'd be."

About The Author

'One of the UK's most promising writers' - *Edinburgh Evening News*

'One of the UK's best talents' - *Lovereading.co.uk*

'Jan Henderson writes the kind of thrillers that make you miss your stop on the bus'- *Times Educational Supplement*

'A moving, funny and original writer' - *The Austin Chronicle*

'Jan-Andrew Henderson has written some incredible books. My favourite author'- Sharon Rooney (*My Mad Fat Diary, The Electrical Life of Louis Wain. Barbie*)

'If there were more books like yours out there, maybe people would be reading more'- Charlie Higson (*Young James Bond* and *The Enemy* series)

Jan-Andrew Henderson (J.A. Henderson) is the author of 40 children's, teen, YA and adult fiction and non-fiction books. He has been published in the UK, USA, Australia, Canada and Europe by Oxford University Press, Collins, Hardcourt Press, Amberley Books, Oetinger Publishing, Mainstream Books, Black and White Publishers, Mlada Fontana, Black Hart and Floris Books.

He has been shortlisted for fifteen literary awards and won the Doncaster Book Prize, The Aurealis Award and the Royal Mail Award - Britain's biggest children's book prize. He runs The Green Light Literary Breakdown Service, teaches online courses for the Romance Writers of Australia Academy and Infostack and has given talks and workshops at festivals, events and schools across the UK and Australia.

He is a professional member of the Institute of Professional Editors, an industry assessor/mentor for the Queensland Writers Centre, a mentor for the Horror Writers Association, an ambassador for Australia Reads, a peer/grant assessor for the Australian Council for The Arts and a convenor for the Aurealis Awards. He features in many anthologies as a contributor and editor and has written several plays - performed as far apart as New York State, Texas, Leeds and the Edinburgh International Festival.

He is also the founder of Black Hart Entertainment, which runs the famous City of the Dead Ghost Tours in Edinburgh.

Naturally, he only wears black.

Chapters

About The Author 5
Chapters 7
Introduction 9
Setting Up 13
The Killer Idea 31
Plot 45
Beginnings 69
Story Mechanics 77
Prose 99
Description 109
Conjuring up Characters 121
Dialogue 143
The Ending 157
Revision 167
Nobody Knows Anything 179
References 195

Introduction

How to Use this Manual

Let's cut to the chase.

If you Google *how to write a story,* you'll find hundreds of articles and websites, many of them containing sound advice and tips. In the same way, there are countless books on novel writing, some of which are extremely insightful.

But they all have flaws. Many are too vague. Some are too busy. A few are a bit pretentious. Others are uninspiring or tell you what anyone who's not an idiot already knows. And, in the future, they're all going to be written by AI Chatbots.

This isn't a guide or a set of musings. It's an instruction manual. It does the same job as the little booklet that tells you how to turn an Ikea flat-pack into a wardrobe. Follow the steps correctly and you end up with a shiny new Umbalplafft.

Unfortunately, I have never built any piece of flat-pack furniture that didn't fall down. That's because I'm impatient and don't like following complicated instructions, so I end up cutting corners.

Bearing these facts in mind, I have tried to make *this* manual as compact and succinct as possible - avoiding a vast amount of literary information that sounds impressive but you don't really need. Just in case you're impatient too.

Let's Write a Page Turner! is comprised of concise nuts and bolts stuff. An attempt to give you solid, practical advice rather than dealing in abstract, floaty concepts. This is the last time you'll see the word 'muse' unless I'm talking about the band.

Common sense is the order of the day. If a bit of advice is vital, I'll include it, no matter how obvious or shop-worn it may seem. Probably more than once. As a counterbalance, I'll caution against sticking to some oft-stated 'rules' if I think they are overrated. I will also throw out some unorthodox ideas that may give you genuine inspiration. Call them tricks if you like. Other authors don't seem to use them but they work and they'll set you apart.

Isn't that what counts?

Official Warnings

I will occasionally do something which I warn everyone who will listen against. Repeat myself. This is a manual, not a manuscript and really important points need to be emphasised more than once. Ditto tips and pieces of advice that are applicable in several places.

Story writing (and teaching) lends itself to a holistic approach but, for the sake of clarity, I have separated some elements that are normally intertwined. Not much use in touting a step-by-step approach if it's one step forwards then two steps back.

Although *Let's Write a Page Turner!* was written to be read from start to finish, some sections can be taken out of sequence (**Dialogue**, **Description** and **Characters**, for instance). **Plot** and **Story Mechanics** are two sides of the same coin and the **Revision** section is worth reading before you write your story, as well as after.

Don't be alarmed or confused. I've never read an instruction manual where I didn't have to go back and check that B and C were slotted correctly into A and D.

Finally, I have included exercises, should you wish to do them. Why not? It's like getting fit. An exercise bike isn't as rewarding as cycling through the countryside and may not actually get you anywhere. But nobody can deny it's good for you.

Why me?

The first thing to ask is, why listen to me? I'm not world famous or even particularly rich. Hey, neither was Van Gogh. Mind you, he was nuts. And a painter.

My main qualification is 25 years of experience in every aspect of writing. I've worked with a range of agents and publishers and written 40 books, from horror to romance, children's novels to adult non-fiction. I've been published by big guns like Collins or Oxford University, specialists such as Amberly Publishers and set up my own press, Black Hart. I've been nominated for a plethora of literary awards, won a few and received glowing newspaper and magazine reviews. Should you wish, you can read the rest in the **About the Author** section. Which, if you're like me, you probably skipped.

If this sounds like I'm blowing my own trumpet, it's because I want you to be confident you're in fairly safe hands.

My other qualification is that I'm a professional editor myself. I see the same mistakes being made over and over and I give the same advice again and again.

I figured I may as well write it down.

Setting Up

Formatting

Let's start with the absolute basics. Why are you writing a book? For people to read. That means you intend to bag an agent, sell it to a publisher or bring it out yourself. Whichever way, it has to be formatted appropriately and you may as well sort that out at the start. If you write by hand, respect. You do you. But eventually, you will have to type it up, so the same advice applies.

There are small variations but, in general, the preferred format is as follows.

Write and save the document as a Microsoft Word file. If any agent or publisher asks for a PDF instead, it's easily converted.
Double or 1.5 line spacing.
A standard font like Times New Roman.
Font size 12.
Standard margins. (usually 2.5 or 2.54)
Insert a page break after each chapter.
Insert page numbers.

No spaces between paragraphs unless it is a deliberate break. I.e. changing POV or shifting to an entirely new scene.

When typing, always use the 'enter' button to start a new paragraph so it can be easily altered.

Indent paragraphs to 0.5 cm or 1.00 cm. You can use 'select all' and then the tabs ruler to indent paragraphs for the whole manuscript, if needs be.

Note. If you end up self-publishing, you will have to change the layout but I'll cover that at the end of the book.

If you don't know how to apply any of these things, just use your preferred search engine. Any number of websites can tell you exactly how it is done more neatly than me. I'll stick to the process of writing.

Be True to Yourself

You are already a writer (even if it's only in your head, so far) or you wouldn't be reading this. I'll assume you know roughly what kind of story you want to tell. If you don't, that's fine. My job is to guide you towards ways of crafting *any* tale and making it unputdownable in the process - if that's even a word.

I'll be using advice from scriptwriters as well as authors, examples from movies as well as short stories and books (if the title doesn't have an author listed alongside, it's one of my efforts). Along with my own experience, I'll touch on what some of the masters of page-turners have to say. You always learn a lot from studying the best, though you don't necessarily have to agree with everything they teach.

That includes me. What I'm giving you is an instruction manual, one that I think works. However, it may not be the way you want to do things. I have a lot of experience but nobody is infallible, so here's my first piece of advice.

Everything I suggest is simply that. A suggestion.

All writing is subjective. If something works for you it doesn't matter if it flies in the face of perceived wisdom. Be true to yourself.

All the same, I would recommend you give the manuscript to beta readers or colleagues whose judgement you respect. They don't have to be writers themselves, just erudite readers. A second or third opinion is always valuable.

Never be put off by criticism unless your gran doesn't like it. Grandmothers are hard-wired to love everything you do, even if it's against the law. If she tells you what you've written is terrible, you best rethink your approach.

But that's for later.

Pick A Genre. Pick any Genre

Throughout this manual are a few scattered observations you don't normally come across in writing guides. They won't appeal to everyone but, trust me, they often work. I want to provide you with new things to ponder rather than lessons you can Google for yourself. No point in me giving examples you've seen and heard a million times.

I may as well plunge in.

Crime. Horror. Romance. Sci-fi. What works for one genre will work for the others.

You may be horrified that I'm lumping those categories together. Many romance writers would argue their work has nothing in common with those of horror meisters. Yet, a novel or short story is like a jigsaw puzzle. The finished picture may be a horrific, exciting or romantic one, yet you assemble the pieces in the same way.

As I said, this is a manual. It works on the same principle as one for building a wardrobe. Or a desk. Or a bed. The finished product may be different but the steps are not and neither are the tools you use.

A page-turner is simply a story you can't put down, whatever the subject matter or genre. It can be deep and meaningful or all style and no substance. Tense and exciting or moving and reflective. It can have serious flaws like Dan Brown's *The Da Vinci Code*. Most critics agree it's poorly written and I'm with them on that. I still thought it was awesome when I read it and so did millions of others. Why?

Because it was a page-turner.

So, pick your genre. Or mix them up and see what happens. Whatever floats your boat. Let's say you decide to write a hard-bitten crime noir. Note two things.

One. You should put the story before the genre every time. If your crime noir begins to turn into a romance or a fantasy, let it. Don't feel you have to be confined to a category just because you started out with it. You're going to hear variations on this sentiment repeated several times throughout this manual, by the way.

Two. Write hard-bitten crime noir because you love it or you have an awesome plot idea. Don't do it because it's a genre you think will sell or is hot right now.

When you get creative, you'll always come across contradictions and dichotomies. Here's another observation that's going to crop up more than once.

No matter how sound a piece of advice appears, it's always worth considering doing the opposite.

I'll give you an example of what I mean. There's a distinction between being restricted and being *deliberately* restricted. No, you don't want to be confined by genre or the market. However, occasionally setting yourself the challenge of staying within distinct parameters works wonders. Writing can be a bit like sex. Sometimes it's fun to slap on a pair of handcuffs.

I was once given a very specific brief to write a short story set in 1970s Krakow. It was to feature James Robertson, a middle-aged photographer with an unspecified genetic disorder which caused him to retire early. On vacation, he was to meet a 40-year-old teacher called Zuzana Wisniewski. What happened next was up to me but it had to have a happy ending.

The result, *The Camera Never Lies*, wasn't the type of story I'd usually tackle - but the brief didn't leave me a lot of wiggle room. Thing is, I loved doing it for that very reason. It forced me to leave my comfort zone and think outside my normal parameters. I was pretty pleased with the result too.

When it comes to genre, there's also a commercial aspect to consider.

With *Spiral Wood*, I set out to write an absolutely typical romance. This was something I'd never tackled before but I'd given myself that challenge and was determined to stick to the script. Then, halfway through, the heroine began to investigate the apparent 'suicide' of a local smuggler.

Now I faced a dilemma. I realised if I went off on a tangent and explored the crime element, I'd have a better story. I'd also have a less commercial one. I went with the crime because I'm more interested in good storytelling than sales figures. I hope you are too, as this manual is about writing, not marketing.

This is something else I'll return to. Don't be afraid to let your story go where it will. If you consider yourself a writer first and a genre writer second, you'll find yourself better at both.

You pick your genre or genres. Or you dispense with categories altogether. What else do you need to contemplate before embarking on your story?

Quite a few things, actually. Some are vital. Some tend to worry writers more than is necessary. All deserve a mention, even if it's just to quickly dispense with them. Like the next one.

Themes

Let's face it. 'Theme' is a pretty abstract concept. Don't get me wrong, it's gratifying if someone reads your story and says *thematically it was rich and mannered with an almost Proustian sense of principality.*

I don't know what that means but some of my author friends actually speak that way and I keep a fly swatter with me at all times to hit them.

The point is, if readers say *thematically it was rich and mannered - everything else about it was rubbish,* you've lost.

Whereas, *I may not have identified any themes but that was a cracking story* is a win.

Don't worry about themes. We all have preoccupations and obsessions and they will come out naturally in your writing. By all means, polish these up when you are finished and make them more obvious. But don't let them get in the way of your story.

I made a conscious effort once to sit down and work out of my books actually had any themes. Turns out almost all of them are about characters who are emotionally stunted and physically or mentally trapped.

I was so depressed I never did it again.

First or Third Person?

Will you write in the first or third person? There are advantages and disadvantages to both.

First Person

This allows you to directly express how your protagonist thinks and feels. On the plus side, it's more immersive and gives the reader real insight into the character. It's especially effective if your hero undergoes a big transformation. (I use hero as a gender-neutral term to describe any main character, by the way).

On the negative side, first-person means you're stuck with them. If something important happens, your main character has to be there. If they aren't around, the scene has to be delivered second-hand. The more intricate the story, the more difficult and annoying this can become (for you and the reader). A first-person approach can also slow your manuscript down if you dwell too much on the hero's internal life.

Third Person.

This is my preferred viewpoint. I like complex plots and I'm naturally guarded, so *Goners* is the only book I've written in the first person. I believe it's easier to write a page-turner if you're not tempted to slow down and tell your audience what the hero thinks all the time. Plus, you can jump around. Different places, varying time periods. That kind of thing.

If you're a beginner, I think third person is easier - but consider the kind of story you are writing and decide which method will work best for you. There's an exercise later on that will help you with this.

Why did I write one book in the first person? I've no idea. I sat down to begin the story and it happened. I'm not advising you do something so cavalier but there's a lot to be said for being spontaneous and following your gut instinct.

Multiple Perspectives

You can also tell your story from the perspectives of several characters. It requires each one to have very distinct characters and voices but, done right, makes for a good ensemble piece (see **A Cast of Thousands**).

Past or Present Tense

Are you going to write in the past or present tense? That's up to you, though I honestly don't understand why so many people write in the present tense. It's not how you talk to your friends and family, is it? Apologies if you do but I find it vaguely pretentious - though that's probably just me. All I know is, if someone tells me a long story in the present tense, I get really irritated.

Yeah. It's probably just me.

Write What You Know

Mark Twain is attributed with saying *write what you know* and many other greats, like F. Scott Fitzgerald, backed him up. Obviously, all writers break this rule at the most fundamental level or there would be no sci-fi and every book would be an autobiography. What they are talking about is sticking to subjects you are familiar with.

Well, that's simply clipping your wings when you want to fly. I'll continue this ungainly metaphor by using a winged creature to introduce an important truth.

Nobody knows anything.

There's an article called *What is it Like to Be a Bat* by the American philosopher Thomas Nagel which illustrates this perfectly. Yes, we're going to be getting into philosophy too.

Nagel states that while we can imagine what it would be like to fly, navigate by sonar, hang upside down and eat insects, we can never understand a bat's perspective. In other words, you don't know what it's like to actually *be* a bat.

By logical extension, you don't know what it's like to be another human being. Not your child. Not your mum. Not your lover. You only know what it's like to be *you*. Everything else is guesswork.

The happy fact is, although we actually know nothing, we have similar basic experiences. Writing about what you know is, in reality, taking a universally understood idea (often a struggle) and making up details to turn it into an original story. This concept will crop up again and again in the manual.

Start with the general and move on to the specifics.

It sounds a bit vague but is really pretty simple. Everyone knows what the universal struggle is. People want things. They try to get them. Stuff gets in their way.

You make up the details. What do they want? Fame? Happiness? A lava lamp? What gets in their way? Mobsters? Lobsters? How will they deal with it? Buckle or persevere? Win or lose? Trample others or help them?

I've written about leaping from a burning building, being on death row, losing a child and encountering a grizzly bear. None of these have actually happened to me, except for the bear, but I know what it's like to feel trapped, lost, despairing and terrified.

God, I've had a shit life.

When I say 'make up' the specifics, I mean exactly that. Unless you are writing a misery memoir, readers don't need to know about your personal issues. They want to enjoy your storytelling skills.

Here's Matt Damon, of all people.

If you are writing a story and trying to draw an audience... it's got to in some way relate to them. Who wants to hear about your specific problems? It's not therapy. It's supposed to be a communal piece of entertainment.

Let's take a concrete example to demonstrate.

Annie Proulx was a seventy-year-old straight woman whose name I had to look up to pronounce properly. In *Brokeback Mountain,* she wrote about the pressures that come about from being true to yourself in the face of societal resistance. That's the generality.

She did it by telling the story of a pair of twenty-year-old cowhands in Wyoming who are condemned by everyone for falling in love. That's the specifics.

We're going to be dealing with those specifics from now on, as they are the building blocks of your page-turner. As Albert Einstein said: *God is in the details.*

All right, he was talking about physics. But that's fine because we'll be delving into quantum mechanics later. Einstein hated quantum mechanics because he didn't quite understand it. And he was bloody Einstein.

See? Nobody knows anything.

While we're at it, a quick check on Google will reveal that Einstein's famous quote was actually coined by the architect Ludwig Mies van der Rohe.

Which brings us neatly to…

Setting and Research

We'll delve into settings more when we come to **Story Mechanics**. For now, I'll touch on the subject because you kind of have to know where your story is going to take place, don't you?

In many cases, you can set a romantic comedy in modern-day Dundee or 20th century Belgrade and have essentially the same story. The only difference is that Belgrade has nicer architecture.

On the other hand, a story can be massively influenced by its setting. A romance between a mixed-race couple, for instance, is going to be hugely different depending on whether you set it in modern-day New York or 1930s Alabama.

The importance of the setting depends on the type of novel you want to produce. If you are writing speculative or historical fiction, it's likely to be fairly integral. Just don't forget this important fact.

The setting, no matter how well rendered, is only background for your story. Unless you are writing a travelogue, don't write a travelogue.

My novel *Secret City* is set in 19th century Edinburgh. I didn't dwell too much on the city itself, though it has an amazing history which I know very well. I merely gave a flavour of it. This allowed me to do things like have a main character develop tuberculosis and be threatened with deportation to Australia. Plot enhancements that couldn't happen nowadays.

I was more interested in the story, which could conceivably have taken place in any city. Google, Wikipedia and a couple of history websites did the trick in developing a background. And don't knock Wikipedia. It isn't 100% right but does the job in most cases. Let me stress that. If your setting really is background, you don't *want* more information than a few websites can provide.

If your setting has more detail than that, it's no longer a backdrop but essential to the story. Sometimes this is the best move and I'll cover it more in the section on **Description**.

If you do feel this is the case, it will require proper research.

You can go the route of R M Ballantyne, who wrote *The Coral Island* in 1857. Getting one fact wrong (the incorrect thickness of coconut shells), he went totally overboard. He stayed at Bells Rock Lighthouse to research *The Lighthouse*, lived with tin miners for *Deep Down* and joined the London Fire Brigade for *Fighting the Flames*.

I don't recommend this.

If you are writing sci-fi or fantasy, you can just make everything up. If it's set in your hometown or another familiar location, you already have everything you need. If your story is historical, or time and location are the focal point of your plot, you better read a couple of reputable nonfiction books on the subject.

However, the same caveats apply. Delving deep into time and setting means you are banking on the reader caring as much about them as you do. Granted, describing a way of life that is fascinatingly alien to most readers ought to keep them hooked. Digging up surprising and little-known facts specific to the location and time will help too. But don't just throw them out there. Work them into the story. Make them obstacles.

Child 44 by Tom Rob Smith is set in Stalinist Russia and is a searing inditement of Soviet-era paranoia, political corruption, the secret police, state orphanages, and homophobia, to name a few. These specific things become the barriers facing the protagonist in his quest for justice.

That's a page-turner.

Exercise 1

Take a chapter or short story of your work which seems to rely heavily on the setting. Rewrite it with the setting somewhere else and in another time (for instance an early 19th century native American village or frontier town). Can the basic story still be told?

Take the place you live and describe it as if you were seeing it for the first time. Try to get the feel of the place, rather than pile on details.

I Think, Therefore I Write

Start with generalities and move on to the specifics. Let's take that up a notch.

Everything I've talked about so far is preparation. What we need now is something more concrete to get us going. And, surprisingly, for such a solid and tangible step, we're going to get all theoretical.

The key to launching your story can be found in philosophy.

I'm not suggesting you read up on metaphysics, delve into the philosophy of language or explore the nature of consciousness - though it's all fascinating.

I'm talking about something simpler, more profound and the perfect starting point.

The philosopher Rene Descartes, which I *can* pronounce, famously said *I think therefore I am*. He arrived at that conclusion by stripping away everything he wasn't completely sure about until he was down to the absolute basics. And the only thing he could be certain about was the fact that he existed.

Cogito ergo sum. I think, therefore, I am.

Then, he began to carefully build on that foundation in order to make sense of the world around him. He got a lot of the subsequent details wrong but that's not what I'm getting at here.

You are going to be creating your own novelistic world and Descartes' example is a fine one to follow. Pare everything down until you reach a small but absolute certainty, then build upon it.

What form will that small certainty take?

We're going to call it the killer idea.

The Killer Idea

The killer idea is the seed from which your story will grow. It's something you are completely certain about. A notion that grabs you and won't let go. Scratches at the corners of your mind until you realize it has to be acted upon.

It can be inspired by anything. Maybe you have a message you want to get across. It might be based on existing or past events in your life. It may revolve around a character you see so vividly you have to tell their story. It could be a twist in search of a plot. You might even come up with a title that tickles you so much you want to fashion a novel around it. Some big-name writers have done just that.

George R R Martin started his whole *Game of Thrones* world domination bid when a vivid opening scene for a novel came to him - finding the dire wolf pups in the summer snows. It was an image he liked and raised interesting prospects. He began to think, *what kind of place snows in summer?*

Then, off he went.

The world is your oyster. A killer idea does not require a theme, revolve around a subject you are familiar with or even need to be a universally understood notion. Just a notion you are passionate about.

How will you build on it? You may not have a clue. Will other people be equally enthusiastic? It doesn't matter. What matters is that you love the concept enough to work on it for weeks or months. Perhaps years.

If you can come up with a completely unique killer idea, my hat is off to you, yet it doesn't have to be something nobody has encountered before. Take romance, for instance. The majority of romance novels have exactly the same central concept - the killer idea for the genre itself.

Girl meets boy. (or boy meets boy, or girl meets girl.). Something gets in the way of their romance. They overcome it. (Or, on rare occasions, they don't).

The generality is exactly the same. Your job is to provide specifics that will make something original out of this well-worn trope. There are a million ways to build on any killer idea and you, obviously, must find your own path.

I'll help by giving a few examples, both from myself and from acknowledged masters of the page-turner. I'll begin with one of the greats: Steven King. He's a fine writer and, more importantly, a constant source of good advice. Here's what he said.

A strong enough situation renders the whole question of plot moot. The most interesting situations can usually be expressed as a What-if *question:*

What if vampires invaded a small New England village? (Salem's Lot).

What if a young mother and her son became trapped in their stalled car by a rabid dog? (Cujo).

These were situations which occurred to me, which I eventually turned into books. In no case were they plotted, not even to the extent of a single note jotted on a single piece of scrap paper.

The killer idea can be as skeletal as that. It's not a story. It's merely the launch pad for your story. Note that King hints at ditching plot entirely, something we will cover in the next section - helpfully titled **Plot**.

Where will *your* killer idea come from?

You can sit and think until you come up with something, which I highly recommend. Or be prepared for it to pounce in the most unexpected moments. Here's where two of mine appeared.

I was walking alongside the Dean River in Edinburgh, staring into the abyss. Pondering, as I'm sure we all do, how much simpler life was when I was a teenager.

I thought: *What if I woke up one day and I was a teenager again?* I wasn't thinking in terms of writing a story. I was simply musing. But, of course, that's where my mind automatically went.

Nah. That body swap stuff had been done to death (*Big. Freaky Friday*), so I began to consider variations. What if I was still an adult but *believed* I was a teenager? That still didn't enthuse me.

What if I woke up and believed I wasn't a younger version of myself but a completely different teenager?

Getting there! Now I needed some obstacles.

What if I was convinced I had done something terrible but couldn't remember what it was? So, I went on the run. Good. I'd be struggling to overcome my paranoia and have to ditch my mobile phone (often a factor in modern stories)

Then I hit on it. What would happen if my estranged teenage son came with me? How would we interact? What bonds might be formed or broken? Where the hell I was going to take all that was beyond me - but I knew it was my killer idea. It became *Waiting For the Train That Never Comes.*

On another occasion, I was working as an Easter Bunny in a mall in Texas, dressed up in a giant pink furry suit that completely obscured me. I swear, I'm not making this up. I became almost non-existent as a person to passers-by. People would have intimate conversations in front of me, as if I were actually a giant rabbit rather than a human being. Slowly an idea formed, which became the novel *Hide*. What if people *did* forget about you? So much that they didn't remember meeting you a few hours afterwards? I couldn't get the notion out of my mind. That's when I knew there was a book in it.

I later found out the same concept was used in an episode of *Star Trek* but it didn't matter. I was taking it in a completely different direction. So, once again, I stress that your killer idea doesn't have to be original. It's just the first building block to something that is.

Yesterday I watched a straight-to-DVD movie called *The Drone*. It was absolutely dreadful, low-budget piffle but the blurb hooked me (there's a lesson to be learned there, which we'll cover when we get to **Synopsis and Covering Letter**). A newlywed couple are terrorised by a drone that has become sentient with the consciousness of a deranged serial killer.

That's simply a variation on the film *Child's Play*, which is a variation on *The Exorcist*. But none of that matters because it's a serial killer in a drone and there's no way I wasn't going to watch that.

In fact, you can use second-hand killer ideas to your advantage. The movie *Pulp Fiction* has two of the oldest tales in the book. The boxer who is supposed to throw the fight but doesn't and the gangster who has to escort the wife of a mob boss but can't touch her.

With these old chestnuts, we know what's meant to happen and it's thrilling when our expectations are subverted. It's a clever move to hang out with a couple of hitmen rather than have them only appear to kill someone. That manoeuvre was so nifty it became a trope of its own - watch *Kraftidioten* (remade as *Cold Pursuit*) or *In Bruges*. Despite the borrowing, all are fantastic films.

Your killer idea does not have to be exciting or original. What you do with it is the important factor.

As David Lynch says:

Don't worry if it has all been said before. Sure it has, but not by you.

Don't sell yourself short, though. You may as well aim high. *The Great Gatsby* has a killer idea that is simple, universally understood and utterly original.

If you desperately want something, you'll never be happy until you get it. But if you do, it won't live up to your expectations and you'll never be happy.

This is an emotional catch-22 of epic proportions and, astonishingly, I can't think of any novel using it before. Feel free to enlighten me if I'm not correct but it doesn't really matter. It's F. Scott Fitzgerald's incredible prose, characters and dialogue that make it a true masterpiece.

Incidentally, the killer idea for Joseph Heller's novel *Catch 22* was so exceptional it entered the English lexicon.

A paradoxical situation from which an individual cannot escape because of contradictory rules or limitations.

Watch More Movies

You'll have noticed by now I'm using films for examples rather than books. There are several reasons for that.

When you ask successful novelists for their number one tip, *read books* is always top of the list. That's a no-brainer, of course, and I wholeheartedly agree. Yet here's my next controversial observation - a counterargument, if you like.

Watch more movies.

Good books are for enjoyment. You can certainly learn masses from them. If a novel is a true page-turner, however, you'll miss important stuff because you're too engrossed in the story. Which is as it should be.

So, I use a lot of examples from movies. I do it because the concepts and steps involved are basically the same. But a movie is short. A shorthand book, if you like. You can get through three movies a day, and it is easier to analyse what they get right and wrong.

Study them dispassionately. Deconstruct them. See how characters are portrayed and dialogue used (movies are especially good for analysing these particular aspects). A good story is a good story. I've said that what works or doesn't work is not dependent on the genre. Often it's not dependent on the medium either.

Writers tend to exist in their own category bubble, refusing to engage with other genres or formats. Burst it. Take inspiration from any sources you can in order to stand out. Remember, the best script writers for film and TV today are the equal of any novelist.

There's also a very mundane reason for referencing movies rather than novels. Scenes from many of the movies I mention can quickly be found on YouTube rather than you having to buy a whole book.

Hey. I'm trying to save you money here.

There's a last justification for choosing movies as examples. They are directed as well as written. A great director can take a bog-standard story and turn it into something wonderful. You can, as well, using the same tricks.

You are not just the writer of your story. You are the director as well.

Obviously, you can't wow with unusual camera angles or multiple light filters. However, you do have some cool moves at your disposal and I'll cover a few of them later. Here's the quick version for now.

As you write, imagine your story as a movie. Visualise every scene as you go. Juxtapose those scenes in a dramatic way to create tension. Figure out when to cut away from a scene for maximum effect. Introduce characters in a dramatic fashion. Experiment with non-linear narrative. Incorporate flashbacks (see **Back Stories**) and move them around to see where they are most effective. Use symbolism, context and imagery to create something unforgettable. (See **Parting Is Such Sweet Sorrow**)

Don't just let the readers *see* what you are putting on paper. Let them see it from the perspective you choose.

In *Waiting For The Train That Never Comes*, I sympathised entirely with Gordon Belin, a man who suffers a nervous breakdown and becomes convinced he is a teenager. More likeable as a big kid than as an adult, he is lost, lonely, confused and desperate for friendship. But I told the story from the perspective or his son Bobby. In Bobby's eyes, this large unstable man is an unpredictable, frightening and hostile rival.

In *Spiral Wood,* the protagonist, Dark Arrowsmith, has an ex-lover and a new flame. Dark knows they are the same man (it makes sense, trust me) but the story is carefully constructed so the reader doesn't.

Now… I could have revealed that information at the beginning of the book and neither the killer idea nor the plot would have changed a jot. But the novel would be a very different beast. The mystery element would have vanished, leaving what I'd consider a rather dull love story. So I directed or, rather, misdirected it.

A last word on movies. Yes, they are very useful tools but they are *not* books. In *Spiral Wood* I was able to keep the giant twist for the very end of the novel by giving deliberately vague descriptions of the love rivals. In a movie, the game would be up as soon the audience saw both men were being played by the same actor.

The Rough Draft

The first draft of anything is shit.

Ernest Hemingway

You've got your killer idea and mulled over how to present it. Whether you have a rough notion of where it's going or a specific plan (See **Plotters and Pantsers**), don't fart around. Take the plunge and get going. Begin a rough draft.

You won't like it. No authors do. It's like launching yourself into rough seas in a boat you haven't checked, with not enough provisions and half a map. Unlike this terrible analogy (by now, you will have realised I am the master of pointlessly convoluted analogies), getting it wrong won't kill you. Don't be scared. Bash it down.

There seem to be two schools of thought on the rough draft. Here's the comedian and writer/director Jordan Peele.

When I'm writing the first draft I'm constantly reminding myself that I'm simply shovelling sand into a box so that later I can build castles.

For a different take, here's best-selling author Dean Koontz.

The danger of planning to do several drafts lies in the subconscious or unconscious attitude that, If I don't get it right this time, it's okay; I can work it out in a later draft. This encourages carelessness in your original word choices, phrasing, and plotting if you write with this approach in mind. No financially successful, critically acclaimed writer I know has let himself get caught in the 'fix it in a later draft' trap. Without fail, however, the hopeless amateur clings to this fallacious theory like a drowning man to the only rock in the lake.

Strong stuff, though it does continue my cliched sailing simile.

Yet, while I appreciate the sandbox analogy, which is better than any of mine - I'm with Dean Koontz. I've edited writers who are on their 25th draft and I really don't see what they are hoping to achieve that hasn't happened in the last 24. Of course, you have to change things. But that's just getting bogged down.

Once I start writing my story, I plough through it. I like to write off the cuff and reckon my first draft - when I'm feeling positive and spontaneous - is probably the best.

I always make major changes to my stories. Huge, totally-alter-the-plot changes. And I do them as I go along. I may jump back and alter a few things but the momentum is always forward. Fast forward.

At the moment, I'm helping my seven-year-old daughter with her reading. She often stumbles over words, slowly spelling them out. I tell her to read faster, which sounds counterintuitive. Things is, she then begins to gloss over the harder words. It means she doesn't pronounce or even understand some of them properly. Yet the sentences come out faster, she gets a better overall sense of the story, gains confidence in her ability and enjoys reading more.

I think people should write the same way. Get it down. Plough on. Keep it moving. Work it out as you go along.

If you have a brilliant idea for a plot development, scene or chapter you want to happen later in your story, resist the impulse to write it. Because you will have to shoehorn it in later and that can be clumsy. Keep it in your head until the time comes to use it. That way, it remains flexible and malleable and will fit better. Don't worry. If something really is good, you'll remember the core details. If you forget them, sorry, but it means they're forgettable.

So here's my next tip.

Don't write scenes out of order. Start at the beginning and continue right through to the end.

It's an approach some authors shun unless they are supremely confident and valiant - or an idiot like me.

But this is a manual and I think following the simplest construction process - start to end - is the best and easiest way to complete your story. When you build an Ikea wardrobe, you don't think: *I'll just go back and put the floor in later*. Besides, all stories are some sort of journey (more of that soon), so why would you jump around? Go on that journey. Your readers have to, so why shouldn't you?

The important thing is you've actually started. You have your killer idea, which will naturally lead you to our next section. The plot.

Now… be prepared to abandon both.

Plot

Writing controlled fiction is called plotting. Buckling your seatbelt and letting the story take over, however... that is called storytelling. Storytelling is as natural as breathing; plotting is the literary version of artificial respiration.

Stephen King

A plot is just one thing after another, a what and a what and a what.

Margaret Atwood.

I'm going to introduce a major point here. In my opinion, there are four main players when it comes to crafting a page-turner. I'll call them the Fab 4 because I can't think of a better title. They are prose, character, dialogue and plot. We'll be tackling the others later but let's begin with plot.

What is a plot anyway? Atwood's 'just one thing after another' is pretty on the nose, if a little world-weary.

I like writing really complex stories but that's a personal preference. The sequence of events making up a plot can be resolutely linear and straightforward. Look how many people are hooked on video games where you follow a bunch of clues, solve a few puzzles and kill all the bad guys. It may sound unoriginal plenty of folk find them exciting, immersive and challenging.

So, let's delve into Plotology (not to be confused with Proctology), the completely made-up science of how to construct a storyline.

Trying something that's totally off the wall might get you prizes or condemnation, though you have my admiration if you try. However, a plot is usually a journey undertaken by the main characters from one point to another. I'm not just talking about getting from New York to Texas.

It *can* mean physical distance. It can also be a journey to solve a problem or escape a foe or rob a bank. This is the narrative arc.

It can also be a journey of self-discovery or one that changes the mindset or perspective of the characters. This is, unsurprisingly, called the character arc.

Both are vital to writing a page-turner.

Narrative and Character Arcs

My favourite kinds of stories are the ones that have these big crazy genre hijinks and then a real honest, meaty, emotional story where we're watching a character grapple with some real things.

Greg Pak

The narrative arc is the characters' physical journey from the beginning of the story to the end. An engaging one flows organically. Each step is an incident that makes the reader want to know what happens next and leads naturally to the subsequent one. Individual scenes eventually add up to a satisfying whole as the plot is resolved.

A character arc deals with the characters' journey from one mental state to another. They learn. They change. They grow.

Don't get too hung up on all the possible permutations of plot incidents. Just make sure each individual scene has a bit of drama, excitement or emotion and you're fine. An argument. A revelation. A moment of reflection. A twist. A chase. A sex scene. A betrayal. A misunderstanding. Clearing up a misunderstanding.

Same with the character arc. Strictly speaking, your heroes don't *have* to learn, change or grow. Frankly, I think it's a pretty old-fashioned way of looking at things. The screenwriter David Fincher says: *I like characters who don't change. Who don't learn from their mistakes.* While *Seinfeld* became one of the most popular TV shows of all time with the maxim *no hugging, no learning.*

But publishers like it when characters do change and grow - especially the major presses. Also, if you're writing kids or YA books, it's pretty much de rigueur.

Don't sweat it. Simply existing usually involves some kind of change, unless you sit in a darkened room forever, refusing to interact with anyone. Then you'll go nuts, which is a character arc in itself.

If you have involving enough circumstances, change will happen. *The Strangler Vine* by M.J. Carter has a cool mystery, fast pace, riveting descriptions of a lost India and vivid characters. Into this promising scenario strides the hero, a complete dick who finds his prejudiced, stuck-up assumptions challenged at every turn.

Here's the important thing. At the end of the book, the hero is still an arse. Just not quite as much as he was at the beginning. So he gets a sequel where he changes a tiny bit more.

When it comes to the crunch, one aspect of the story arc - be it narrative or character - is all important. Neither journey should be a straight line.

The greater the physical, emotional or mental obstacles thrown in the hero's way, the better. The more ingenious or thrilling or harrowing their attempts to surmount these obstructions, the more a reader will want to read on. As the famous film director Alfred Hitchcock once said:

Make the audience suffer as much as possible.

You can't root for a hero if all they have to do is complete a round of golf - unless it's across a minefield. I'm not saying high stakes have to mean life or death. If they are important to the character and the writer sells the validity of that belief, readers will be hooked. In a page-turner, whether two star-crossed lovers will end up together should be just as nail-biting as whether the hero will catch the killer.

Obstacles

Make the audience suffer.

The worse the odds for your main characters, the more tense and exciting the read and the more satisfying it is when those obstacles (mental or physical) are overcome.

Start with generalities and move to specifics.

Obstacle-wise, your heroes may find themselves faced with a dreadful realisation or an impossible choice. That's the generality.

A mother may discover her daughter has killed someone and have to decide whether to turn her in. That's the specifics.

Here's an example from *Gone Baby Gone* by Dennis Lehane. Private Detective Patrick is hunting a missing girl. His dreadful realisation is that she was kidnapped by his friend, retired police chief Doyle, who believes the kid is better off with him than her drug-addled mother. Now Patrick has an impossible choice.

You don't want Patrick to turn his friend in. The girl doesn't want him to. The woman he loves tells him she'll leave if he does. Even Patrick doesn't want to do it. However, a crime has been committed and a mother separated from her child. So Patrick obeys the law and does the 'right thing'. Doyle goes to prison, Patrick's happiness is ruined and so is the life of the girl he 'rescued'.

I use this example for another reason. Patrick doesn't overcome his final obstacle. However, you could give exactly the same story a happy ending simply by having him walk away. You have to be open to any possibility. Mentally venture down every fork in the road. God is in the details.

I bet Lehane thought about both before picking the hauntingly tragic ending. Watch the movie version. It will scar you forever. Yet, why would you aim for anything less?

Which leads us to the way you structure your story.

Planners, Pantsers and Failed Plotters

You have a killer idea and are about to begin your journey. You're going to have a sequence of events and put in obstacles for the protagonists to overcome. Obviously, I don't know what they are. The question is, do you?

Before we get going, it's best to know what kind of plotter you are

Planners

You can plan your novel meticulously before you begin. Work out the beginning, middle, end and all the twists and turns in between. Refuse to begin your journey without knowing exactly how to get to where you're going and what's going to be in your hero's way. This allows you to write fluently and efficiently and concentrate on your craft, knowing you're not going to get stuck halfway through. It sucks to begin with as you struggle with what fits where. After that, it should be relatively plain sailing.

I have never been able to do it.

Pantsers

You can be a Pantser (a term I utterly loathe, by the way). Start off with not much more than the killer idea and see where the hell it goes. This will cause your brain to explode several times and bring you to the edge of a nervous breakdown. But it allows you to adapt as you go and it's a more exciting way to write.

I'll go back to Steven King, who puts it in even stronger terms.

I believe plotting and the spontaneity of real creation aren't compatible.

Sometimes the first image or idea that we write down is, in fact, a gateway to a deeper or more specific notion, a better place the story can go. If we hold on tightly to the core idea, we will never allow ourselves to venture where we could. Hold your ideas loosely. Do not become too attached to what 'must' happen.

As you can see, King is not just applying this advice to a prototype plot but the killer idea as well. Don't be afraid to let it go completely if you stumble across something more appealing in the process.

After all the effort you've put in it, not to mention reading three sections of this manual, abandoning everything you've done may fill you with horror. Which is why I recommend the following compromise.

Failed Plotters

There's a third option which I tend to use. That of the failed plotter.

From my killer idea, I will sometimes work out a pretty detailed plot. I'll start writing that detailed plot and absolutely nothing will go as planned. Every new idea leads to another new idea until my original train of thought has been well and truly derailed.

That's the joy of writing, after all. Unleashing your imagination. If you see a more exciting and rewarding path opening up, you have to follow it. Even if it seems to lead in the opposite direction from the one you intended to take.

My killer idea for the novel *The Kirkfallen Stopwatch* was of a pregnant woman smuggling diamonds in a bag in her stomach. When the plane crashes, the diamonds become fused into her unborn baby's skin - making the child a target for every reprobate under the sun.

Absolute B-Movie tosh, you'll agree, but I felt there was a real emotional core to explore.

Suitably fired up, I began writing, only to find the story was transforming into something completely different. It ended up being about an island full of psychopaths, a research facility overrun by ants, a double killing in an idyllic community and a mass murderer hunting his own daughter - all part of the greatest con in history. *None* of these were in my original vision. What I did have simply vanished as I saw where a superior story could emerge.

I've said the killer idea is something you are absolutely certain about. I've said you are creating a novelistic word, which makes you a little god (See **You Are a Little God**). But Gods and philosophers can be wrong. Sometimes you have to step back and let the plot simply... evolve. Accept it may evolve into something unrecognisable.

I promised I'd do the best I could to provide practical advice. Now I've suggested the very foundations I asked you to build your story on are shaky ones. At this crucially fluid stage, you need *something* concrete to hold on to.

And that's the ending.

The plot is a journey and all journeys have a destination. It's important to know where you are going, so this is what I suggest.

Always work out a rough ending for your story before you start writing. It may end up nothing like the eventual ending but, initially, it gives you something to aim for.

We'll refine this when we get to the section on **Endings**. For now, a rough idea will do.

Why and What If

> *Everything's always about page turning, right? What's next? So, if you create questions for audiences, then they'll want to know the answer. Or they begin to formulate possible outcomes. That's the game we play when we're hearing a story unfold.*

Ron Howard

I said the key to launching your story can be found in philosophy. Guess what?

The key to building your plot is also found in philosophy.

What do you say to someone with a philosophy degree? "I'd like a big Mac and fries, please."

I can make that joke because I do have a philosophy degree, so I know it's a field that can be boiled down to asking the same question repeatedly. *Why?*

Kids are great at it. Here's the exchange between John Candy and McCauley Culkin in *Uncle Buck*. That's right. *Uncle Buck*.

Where do you live?
In the city.
Do you have a house?
Apartment.
Own or rent?
Rent.
What do you do for a living?
Lots of things.
Where's your office?
I don't have one.
How come?
I don't need one.
Where's your wife?
Don't have one.
How come?
It's a long story.
Kids?
No I don't.
How come?
It's an even longer story.

From a writer's point of view, this tells us a great deal about Uncle Buck and the kid in a short space of time – which is great. However, the point I'm making is that plot is all about questions and answers. And the two most important questions are *What if?* and *Why?*

What if? and *why?* are the building blocks of your page-turner. They set up the story and the readers keep reading to find out the answer. It's that simple.

Of course, nothing is *that* simple. You can't just throw out a few generic setups using boring questions and perfunctory answers. Start with generalities and move on to specifics.

What if two people fell in love? That's too general. Ideally, your *what ifs* should be surprising, intriguing, emotional or powerful. What if a cleaning lady fell in love with a fish man in a tank? (*The Shape of Water*). What if two students fell in love but one developed a terminal illness. (*Love Story*)

If you have initial intriguing *what ifs*, the *whys* and the answer to those *whys* will result in a fulfilling progression of events. Now we throw in a few more *what ifs* as obstacles with *whys* to elaborate.

What if this goes wrong? Why would it go wrong? (General).

What if he can't reach the bridge? Why can't he reach the bridge? (Specific).

What about the answers to *why* and *what if?* The need to be of the same calibre as the questions. If your solutions are exciting or emotional or surprising enough, you've completed a home run.

Let me put it as a formula because that looks suitably scholarly.

Intriguing* what if? + *plausible* why? + *dramatic solution* = *page-turning plot.

If we repeat this formula while raising the stakes each time, we've got the baseline for a thrilling read. To ensure that actually transpires, we have to up our game.

Tease things out and don't give away too much. If you can, keep the reason the protagonists are solitary, unhappy, cursed or on the run until it comes as a surprising revelation. Delay gratification to build up suspense. And here's the most important aspect of all.

A page-turner answers questions in a way that raises more questions.

So Alice shot him! Now we know the killer at last! But wait! CCTV footage shows she was in Budapest at the time. How can that be?

Perfect. You've answered one question and it immediately set up another puzzle to solve.

A variation is the question which could have a number of different possible answers. Agatha Christie's *Murder on the Orient Express* asks which passenger killed Samuel Ratchett, presenting the reader with a number of potential suspects. Note the neat inversion at play here. In order to work out *who* killed him we need to know *why* he was killed. Again there are several possible answers and I won't spoil the ending by telling you it was all of the passengers.

Though *why* and *what if* are the best catalysts for plot building, beware of the obvious drawbacks when you answer. Having some random stranger appear and say *actually, I was playing a prank, so everything is OK* won't cut it.

Teasing the reader by delaying answers is effective in building tension and it's great to keep a big one for near the end. You want keep people hanging on until the finale and finish with a bang.

But there's a line you shouldn't cross. Don't keep back pertinent information that will stop the reader getting confused or lost. Nor should you delay answering questions for so long that they lose interest. Leaving all the answers till the very end might seem clever but usually requires a huge amount of exposition at the very point when the story should be becoming its most thrilling and emotional. Unless you're writing an *Inspector Poirot* novel, sow the questions and answers right through the story.

It's pretty easy to do. Here's a simple progression using *why* and *what if*.

You find yourself in a hotel room with no idea how you got there. *Why* are you there? *Why* can't you remember?

The next move is obvious. You go and look out the door. *What if* the door is locked? You try to get out the window. *What if* the windows are barred?

There's your second chance to thread in a *why*. *Why* does a hotel room have barred windows? Ooooh! The reader wants to know.

Back to the problem at hand. You'll have to break open the door. At this point, we can see both external and internal aspects of this hero's journey developing. Figuring out how they got there and figuring out how to escape (narrative) along with fear and confusion (character). *What if* they can't get out? Then you've painted yourself into a corner and have to provide a solution before the reader gets bored. Also, it's time for a more exciting answer than the common knee-jerk responses you've been providing.

Not a problem. You switch to a larger canvas, the journey expands and the stakes get raised.

What if someone suddenly unlocks the door from the outside? Then he tries to kill you. *Why? What if* he's wearing a hazmat suit and won't come near you? *Why? What if* it's your sister, who you thought was dead? *Why* is she alive? *Why* is she pointing a gun at you?

I've got no idea but I want to know!

There's no exact formula but, by now, you should be getting a fair picture of how to build a plot. Take a killer idea. Begin your journey with a destination in mind. Set up obstacles using questions as barriers.

What if the love of her life gets drafted?

Overcome these obstacles by answering them as the story progresses while always raising more.

He deserts to be with her but how can they live a normal life now?

Save one major question to be answered at the end of your journey.

How can they find a way to be together safely?

Naturally, *what if* and *why* are not the only types of questions you can ask. If you want to be pedantic, there are seven and they're called interrogative words. *Who, what, where, when, why, which*, and *how*.

No prizes for guessing my favourite two, although the others all have a part to play.

Why is she being followed will in itself be followed by *who* is following her? *What* is in the mysterious box and *where* did she find it? *How* was she killed and *when* did it happen? *Which* of the two lovers will she choose?

Once you get started, interrogative words are not just the building blocks but the engine that drives your story along.

While the general concept is easy to follow, the specifics can be a pain. Juggling all these questions and answers means you'll have to keep a dozen possibilities in the air, an analogy that can't be too bad because James Cameron uses the same one.

It's like how many balls can you get in the air at once? All those ideas float out there to a certain point and then they'll crystallize into a pattern.

That pattern can be damned elusive, so I'll switch to a worse analogy. Think of plotting as climbing an impossibly huge tree. Each time you reach a certain height, the branches fork, and you have several potential routes to take. If you come to a point where you can't get any higher, mentally climb down a branch and try another direction. Which… would make your destination the top of a tree.

I'll say it again. Even if you've meticulously plotted your page-turner with graphs and spreadsheets, I urge you to be open to changing the direction of your cherished trip.

There Are No Stupid Questions, Only Stupid Answers

The best solutions don't give readers what they expect. Which isn't the same as not giving them what they want.

We *want* the lovers to get together. We *want* the bad guy to get his comeuppance. We *want* the hero to triumph. These are the outcomes most readers desire, though you don't want getting there to be too obvious. Nothing beats originality but there are some tried and tested methods you can put your own spin on.

You can use a red herring, a device used to divert attention from the truth. In *The Kirkfallen Stopwatch*, the hero is kidnapped by her estranged father. When we learn he is the infamous Houdini Killer, a man who has gone on two separate killing sprees, it doesn't look good for the poor lass. We only find out later the 'kidnapping' is actually a rescue.

You can use a MacGuffin - a term popularised by Alfred Hitchcock in *The 39 Steps*. This is an object, device or event that drives the plot but is irrelevant in itself. In *The 39 Steps*, Richard Hannay becomes caught up with a spy ring attempting to steal military secrets. The content of these 'secrets' are of no importance to the story whatsoever. Hitchcock simply asks the audience to accept they're vital, then follow along in the adventure, as Hannay goes on the run to escape the bad guys.

McGuffins and red herrings are handy devices but today's readers are savvy. If your novel is a whodunnit, for instance, don't throw too much suspicion on a minor character or the reader will suss out that he's definitely *not* the killer. I've lost count of the number of whodunnits where the murderer is the only character with no other reason to be in the book.

How do you get around it? By having another three characters in the story with no apparent reason to be there. Now it could be any of those.

Whenever you can, be subversive and do the unexcepted. In a detective team, the partner weeks away from retirement will die. Make it the young one who gets killed instead.

Emotional Responses

In this section, I've talked about questions, answers and obstacles more in terms of narrative than character arc. Yet the two are intrinsically tied and their guiding principles are the same. In terms of plot, one thing happens, which causes another thing to happen, which causes another. In terms of character, they make a choice that leads to a consequence, which leads to another choice leading to another consequence.

Then it's just a case of revealing what the sequence of events will do to the protagonists. What will their emotional response be? What moral consequences will they face? How will it change them?

Tweak the *what ifs* and *whys* so the physical journey has a mental counterpart. Will your hero triumph or fail? What is the cost for either outcome? Will they emerge unscathed or damaged? If they win, will they have doubts about the price of their victory?

In many ways, the character arc is easier to navigate than the narrative arc and the clue is in the name.

Remember the Fab 4? Plot, prose, dialogue and character? If you get the protagonists right, they'll supply the emotional heft for you. Remember, the best plot in the world will have no impact if you don't care about the people caught in its web. If your protagonists are realistic, however, they'll practically make their own decisions. We'll come to that more in **Characters**.

Lead your heroes further and further into a physical and mental morass before rescuing them (or not rescuing them).

The task of building a plot from scratch can be daunting. But you are a writer, and writers relish a challenge. At least, that's what I keep telling myself.

Exercise 2

Treat your protagonist's narrative arc as if it really were a physical journey. Draw a map, complete with obstacles and a destination. It doesn't have to be a masterpiece. Even a simple tube map will do.

```
Find path of    Pick up           Wrong train
true love       emotional  Lose the  of thought   Happy Ever
                baggage    plot                   After
─■─○────○────────○────────○────○──────○────○──────○─■
Start with  Take the moral        Cross this bridge  Leap of  Mental
a bang      high ground   Dont even when you come to it  faith  Block
                          go there
```

Getting Stuck.

Voices in your head may say "My story is no good. Writing is too hard. I suck." Here's how you fight them: Write the next sentence.

David Lynch

I went to a talk by an author I know. I won't name her because she'd be pretty annoyed about me telling you this. She said: *If you get really stuck, don't be afraid to abandon the whole book and start again.*

You'll hear this from other authors too, cause it sounds very brave and avant-garde.

In my opinion, it's nonsense. If you get stuck, sit and think. Go to bed and think. Think for weeks if that's what it takes. A solution will eventually come and you'll do a little dance.

I wrote the book *Goners* in two months. *Hide*, on the other hand, took 23 years to finish. I'm not saying I spent all that time thinking about it. I wrote a bunch of stuff in between. I just waited until I had more experience to tackle something so complex, then went back and finally solved the flaws that were vexing me.

Writer's block? It's like a toilet. Just keep poking until it unblocks.

I do understand the feeling of being overwhelmed, however. So many balls to juggle! So many ideas to keep straight in your head! So many avenues to explore! It's all too much.

When you feel like that, step back and study what you have in a scientific way. Then apply Quantum Mechanics.

Oh yes. Quantum Mechanics.

Specifically a concept I call Schrödinger's Butler.

Schrödinger's Butler

I can almost hear you groan. First philosophy. Now Quantum bloody Mechanics. But hear me out.

I'll simplify this massively. On a quantum level, particles are affected by observation. Ernst Schrödinger came up with a hypothetical theory that involved sealing a cat and something minuscule that could kill it (like a radioactive atom) in a box. You don't know if the cat is dead or alive until you open the lid and observe the particle. Until then, the cat is, in a sense, both dead and alive. Quantum Mechanics 101.

Don't worry if you don't get it. As another scientist, Richard Feynman, said:

If you think you understand quantum mechanics, you don't understand quantum mechanics.

The same is true of novel writing.

Is your character a mass killer or have they been framed? Yes and no? Will the star crossed lovers get together? Yes and no? Did the butler do it? Yes and no?

To begin with, either outcome is possible. The same is true of any plot development, circumstance, character or place. Everything in your story exists in a fluid state until you get to the point where you allow the reader to observe it. Like quantum mechanics, creating a tale from tiny unstable particles is a process you can undertake without really knowing how it works.

Which is a good time to introduce *story* mechanics. Story mechanics is not quite plot. It's… well.. mechanics. To use another bad analogy, if plot is the skeleton, story mechanics are the muscles, veins and organs of your writing body. Messier but just as vital to it functioning properly.

Before we get to that, let's take a break and do some actual writing. Get a feel for how you are going to lay out the words.

Let's begin the beginning.

Beginnings

These days attention spans have gotten shorter. Sorry. What was I saying?

Oh yes. There are now plenty of people who, if they don't like a story's beginning, will stop reading. Agents and editors will usually scan the first few pages and go no further if they aren't blown away.

How you write the first two or three paragraphs will be the clincher as to whether people keep reading the first couple of chapters. How you write the first couple of chapters will determine whether they read the rest of the story. In short...

The beginning is the most important part of your story.

The Title

People forget that the title is actually the start of your story. From the conception of your killer idea to the point where you send your manuscript to a publisher (or self-publish), never stop thinking about alternatives to the title. When I'm in a bookshop, I look at the spines and pull out those with the names that intrigue me most. Make the title catchy, original and non-generic. It's true that a publisher may change it. Oxford University Press changed *Waiting for the Train that Never Comes* and *The Kirkfallen Stopwatch* to *Crash* and *Colony*, while Floris Books changed *The Armageddon Twins* to *It's Only the End of the World*.

I simply waited. When the rights eventually reverted to me, I changed them back.

The First Line

First sentences are doors to worlds.

Ursula Le Guin.

If you can think of a dazzling first line, that's a joyful moment. A good one will do, though. I prefer short and pithy with an emphasis on short. Stephen King says:

An opening line should invite the reader to begin the story. It should say: Listen. Come in here. You want to know about this.

That's why *once upon a time* is the standard bearer. Having said that, however, it's actually the first few paragraphs that count.

We've already established that setting up questions early on is a good way to suck in your audience. So is introducing a mystery or puzzle of any sort. You can use sparkling dialogue, a memorable character, a monumental decision or a WTF moment. Go over the first lines and chapters several times until you know you've done the best job you can. Set out your stall and show the reader they're in for a treat.

Here's what to avoid.

One. Don't put in too much description at the beginning.

Two. Don't dwell at length on the setting. Setting a mood is more important.

Three. Don't focus on backstories or jump back and forward in time. Not right at the beginning.

Four. Avoid cliches. People waking up. Dream sequences. The weather or season. What the character looks like.

Four. Don't burden the reader with information they can easily figure out later. Find a later point to reveal this info so that it comes as a shock or a surprise.

In the very beginning, everything should move the plot forward. You can slow things down once the reader is hooked.

Be Bold

Start your book with a bang and it's hard to go wrong. The reader will want to follow that enigmatic/funny/character. Discover why they are in this tense situation, how they escape or how a dramatic scene will play out.

Goners starts with the hero hanging from a fishing crane above a sea filled with killer Humble Squid. There's no explanation but all the initial information the reader needs is in this scene. The setting (an island). The job he does and the situation he is in (he is a lawman and slipped while chasing a fugitive). His character (He admits there's no point in complaining about his fate before ranting about how unfair it is – revealing that he is hypocritical yet witty). It also sets up a bunch of questions. Who is the fugitive? Why is the fugitive running? Why are there killer Humble Squid below when no such creature exists in our world?

Be bold. In the first chapter of *Bunker 10,* the reader is told everyone in the book will die within 24 hours. According to many writers, that's a big no-no. Tough. I wanted to set up a sense of fatal inevitability and that was the way to do it.

Burnt Out is about a couple of disabled teenagers trapped in a burning hospital. With such a small cast, it was vital the reader care about them. So I had the heroes be forced to share a hospital room and hate each other on sight. Then I turned their arguments into a comedy double act.

In a survival adventure, an approach where danger (the fire) doesn't break out until page 50 may seem counterproductive but I tried introducing it earlier and it didn't work as well. Because it was information the reader didn't need. They know what is coming. It's obvious from the cover and blurb that the situation is going to turn deadly. By starting with comedy, I had introduced a contrast which allowed me to leaven an intrinsically sad story.

In *The Kirkfallen Stopwatch,* the first few chapters seem to have absolutely no connection with each other. A research station overrun by ants in the Mohave Desert. A fake psychic investigator looking into a paranormal occurrence in Aberdeen. A boy who suspects a double suicide on his isolated island was actually a murder. A girl in Edinburgh discovering her father is a famous mass killer.

No explanation was offered to link any of these events. How were they all connected? I was betting the reader would keep going to find out.

Be bold.

Prologues.

Prologues have fallen out of fashion. Publishers don't like them, preferring to launch right into the story. They especially hate a prologue that doesn't seem to have anything obvious to do with what follows. Which is kind of the point of a prologue, really.

I find this perplexing, to be honest. I like prologues, *especially* if they seem to have nothing to do with what comes next. If it takes half the book to see where they fit in, that's fine by me. *Hide* begins with a herd of cattle walking off a cliff and the explanation as to why doesn't occur for a couple of hundred pages.

Thing is, I don't hear any readers complaining about them. It's good to start a page-turner with a shock or puzzle. So here's a bit of antagonistic advice.

Put in a prologue. Hell. Put in two.

Also, a prologue gives your prospective editor something to do. They'll usually tell you to cut it, which you can generally do without changing the book much. Then they feel they've suggested something constructive and they're happy.

If you genuinely want to keep it, don't call it a prologue. Call it Chapter One.

We'll go back to story mechanics in a second but the next exercise is obvious.

Exercise 3

Take the first chapter of your book or the first two pages of your short story. If it is narrated, tell it from the point of view of a character. If it is from a point of view, narrate it. If it is in the first person, change it to the 3rd person or vice versa. Same with past and present tense.

This is not a fruitless endeavour. You'll be going back to the beginning after the next few sections so you can apply what you've read. In fact, you should go over the beginning several times as your story progresses, refining, polishing and, possibly, restructuring it.

Don't lose your reader at the first hurdle. It's your literary Custer's last stand. Only at the beginning. And where Custer wins.

Told you I was bad at analogies.

Story Mechanics

Start with generalities and move on to the specifics. You have killer idea. A basic journey with an ending in sight. A sequence of events made of questions and answers and obstacles to overcome. A beginning.

Now we add in organs and veins to the skeleton of our awful analogy to get the heart pumping.

All of the following ingredients are going to play a part in your story. Some haven't been mentioned before. Others we are briefly revisiting. All of them are easy to master by following straightforward guidelines. If we were building a wardrobe, these would be the shelves.

Sorry. That was another terrible analogy and I should slap myself with a wet haddock. As I said, I am the absolute master of crappily convoluted analogies, which is probably why there is no section on them.

The Setting

I touched on the setting before but I have a few more thoughts to add now that we are on our way.

As we established, settings can play a background role or be an integral part of your story. In either case, the same advice applies.

No matter how fascinating the surroundings, don't go on about them.

My favourite place is Venice, which is astonishing in every single way. Yet if I get out my holiday pictures and tell you about it in great detail for hours, you'll be bored to tears. Show a place to the reader gradually, rather than tell them about it. (See **Show Don't Tell**). This applies to intricate, made up worlds too. Start with a piece of action that demonstrates how this world works without going into too much detail. Once the reader is on board, you can dial the pace back and begin to portray it properly.

If you feel your world is so complex you have to offer a thorough and encompassing overview right away? Put it in a prologue.

If you're staying on earth and are familiar with an exotic location, consider ways to work it in. Everyone likes to go to glamorous places. Conversely, don't be afraid to set the book in the place you know best - your hometown. So what if it's dull and suburban? You know it well and 99.999% of the world's population has never been there. That's exotic enough for most people.

I live in a suburb called Bellbowrie which is nicknamed 'Bellboring'. Would I set a novel there? Sure. I've seen David Lynch's *Blue Velvet*.

Having a romance take place on the Cote D'Azur or Paris in the springtime means the location is going to a lot of the heavy lifting. But it's also a bit cliched. Setting a gritty drama in a Glasgow slum or a caravan site in Skegness is much the same.

What you want to consider is playing around with these staples. A romance about an out of work plumber from a Glasgow slum on vacation in Paris is an opportunity to cover fresher ground.

Yes, setting is crucial. But actual location is only a part of setting and describing one will only generate so much interest. It's the people who live there that count.

Setting is less important than society.

Many great sci-fi novels have incredible worldbuilding. But it's the way their society works that makes the story and society is made up of interesting characters doing dramatic things.

If two people meet somewhere, briefly describe the location, always bearing in mind that what the reader really wants is the characters interacting. Put that off too long while you dwell on the colour of the hotel curtains and you'll lose their interest.

Symbolism.

I've talked about the writer also being the director of their story. Directors love symbolism. It's adding depth and gravitas with the flick of a literary switch.

Symbolism can change the mundane into something unforgettable.

I think one of the greatest speeches in novel or film is from *Bladerunner*. The critic Mark Rowlands described it as *perhaps the most moving death soliloquy in history.*

After a ferocious battle, the 'bad guy' (Roy Batty) is standing over the 'hero'(Deckard) - who is hanging from scaffolding. The dying Batty can finally get revenge on the man who hunted his friends down. Yet, his final action is to pull Deckard to safety and deliver these lines.

I've seen things you people wouldn't believe. Attack ships on fire off the shoulder of Orion. I watched C-beams glitter in the dark near the Tannhäuser Gate.

All those moments will be lost in time, like tears in rain.

Time to die.

Sounds like a bit of science fiction codswallop, doesn't it? Until you add the magic ingredient of symbolism.

Batty stands, almost naked, arms crossed like a vengeful God, watching Deckard's doomed attempts to save himself. At the last moment, Batty reaches out to grasp Deckard and we see he has a nail through his hand. Then he expires, releasing the dove he has been holding.

There are other symbols at play here (The aftermath of a biblical flood. God reaching out to Adam. Rain substituting for tears) but the main one is inescapable. We realise this android is a Christ symbol and his last act is one of selfless grace. He has died for the sins of humanity and, in rescuing his mortal enemy, revealed he is better and more forgiving than them.

Meanwhile, Deckard realises, to his horror, that *he* has been the bad guy all along. This is his own small redemption and a quantum shift in perception for the audience.

It's completely unforgettable.

Back Stories

> *I don't really come up with years' worth of background story for each character. I tend to jump very quickly into specific situations. First, I really think of the surface actions they would do in the story. Then meanwhile I continue thinking about, well then who are the characters?*

Bong Joon Ho

We've talked about two parallel strands to your story - narrative and character arcs. There's also another set of parallels at work. The 'front' and 'back' story. The front story is what's happening on the page right now. The back story (or backstory) is what occurred in the past.

Front story is self-explanatory but back story varies. It may be huge and all-encompassing. In sci-fi, it can be what brought an entire civilization to the point where the front story is being told. It can be small and intimate - what brought your characters to the dating app where they meet.

Used right, it's great for clarifying storylines and making readers sympathetic (or hostile) to characters. As in real life, every character has a backstory. It's up to you to decide how much of it you want to divulge.

I'd treat it the same way as description. Use backstory but don't overdo it or simply plonk information down. Weave back stories into the main tale and use them to enlighten the reader. To explain motivations or shed light on present circumstances. Only include it when the reader *needs* to know about past events.

How best to work in backstory? There are a few main ways.

One. You can use flashbacks. These can be long or short. Frequent or infrequent. In Joseph Conrad's *Heart of Darkness*, a flashback takes up almost all of the narrative.

When I say work in flashbacks, I don't mean throw them in willy-nilly. I recommend putting them as separate sections or chapters to avoid any possible confusion as to what is happening and when.

And never change tenses in the middle of a back *or* a front story.

Two. Past events can come out in conversation. Watch the USS Annapolis scene in *Jaws* for a masterclass - as a fun conversation about scars develops into a chilling story (see **Take Time Out Occasionally**). Note the symbolism. Though they're talking about physical scars, the conversation is far more revealing about mental scars.

It's hard to sustain that level of writing, so I would use conversations about the past sparingly and only in short bursts.

Three. A narrator (or the writer) can narrate. This works best for fantasy and sci-fi epics, where you have a lot to establish. The opening script in *Star Wars* scrolls across the screen and sets up a whole universe in only a few seconds.

This does not work so well anywhere else.

It's easy to reveal past events by narration but also clumsy. If you must impart a slab of backstory, flashbacks work better. Why? Because the one thing you must always do is show, not tell.

Show Don't Tell

Part of the writer's bible, really. Also, a very easy instruction to follow.

If you have a protagonist attacked by a shark, show them being attacked by the shark (even if it has to be in flashback). Don't tell us about them being attacked. Don't have them tell us about being attacked. Don't have anyone else tell us about being attacked. Show it.

Of course, there are always exceptions. You can 'tell' if an action is short and inconsequential.

A bee stung me in the eye once. It swole up and I could hardly see.

You can 'tell' if you are hiding something from the reader or another character. In a crime thriller, you're not going to show the killer murder someone if his identity is meant to be a mystery.

You can 'tell' if a vital piece of information *has* to be imparted and there's a lot of action going on. Just bear in mind that fast-moving sequences are not the time to be getting into details.

But, in the main, if a scene is dramatic, exciting or long, the reader doesn't want to hear about it second hand. They want to see it!

Show don't tell applies to characters too. As Nagle stated, we don't know what it's like to be another person. You may think you know your best friend or partner inside out but you're not in their head. Fictional characters are the same. If you want to create a page-turner, concentrate on what they say and do and less on what they think. If a character is afraid or hurt, do not say *I was terrified* or *I was devastated*. Make them tremble or burst into tears instead.

Again, I'll go back to my preoccupation with movies. When I'm writing a novel, I see it as a film in my head. I dream up the dialogue and direct the action. Then I simply write down what I'm seeing.

Show, don't tell.

Pace and Tension

Pace is the speed with which events happen in your story. If your scenes drag, you'll bore readers. If the pace is too fast, the story will feel rushed and bitty.

Tension is the element that evokes worry, anxiety, fear or stress (for both reader and character, hopefully). Sustained tension is similar to too fast a pace. It's a thrill ride but doesn't leave room for emotional development and you won't remember much of it.

Guides often advise writers to remove scenes that aren't pertinent to the plot or don't advance the story. This is sound enough advice - don't ramble on endlessly about what the protagonist had for lunch. But if you think up a scene that is funny or poignant, even if it's not relevant, I say keep it in. (See **Take Time Out Occasionally**).

My editor told me to remove a chapter from *The Armageddon Twins* where the hero dresses as a clown to fight a loan shark.

"There's no need for it," she said. "It just slows the pace down."

True. I also thought it was really funny, so I insisted it be kept in. One newspaper review said: *The clown scene is genuinely inspired*. Score one for me.

What you want to avoid is a non-pertinent scene, explanation or screed of dialogue when the book is moving along swiftly. Save these for downtime moments when not much is happening. Then you can take time to let the reader get to know your characters or setting.

Treat your story like a roller coaster ride. Slow increase of tension, worry and stress (going up). Fast-paced release in a burst of action or dramatic moment (going down). Then a quiet pause for reflection before starting up again.

Plus, in my case, a lot of screaming.

Chapter Endings

> *I end each chapter with a cliff-hanger, resolution, a turn, a reveal, a new wrinkle ... something that will make you want to read the next chapter of that character.*

George R R Martin

This applies more to novels, really. End every chapter with a cliffhanger. Old matinee serials were on to a neat trick when they did it - and if it's good enough for *Doctor Who*...

I don't mean each chapter should have a protagonist literally hanging off a cliff, though it couldn't hurt. I don't even mean it figuratively. Chapter endings don't need to feature monumental life or death situations, just a powerful moment, question or revelation. A reason to flip to the next chapter rather than put the book down and go feed the cat.

If you can't think of a dramatic ending to your chapter? End your chapter at the next dramatic moment you write.

It Was a Dark and Stormy Night

Many writers are big on foreshadowing. This is typically phraseology that alludes to future events and can be subtle or obvious.

It was a dark and stormy night suggests, for instance, that something bad is going to happen. For cliché spotters, if a detective is approaching retirement day, you can bet he's not going to reach retirement day. I've lost count of the number of books prophesying 'The One'- which is as overt as you can get. And I'm sick to death of them.

There's a very large school of thought which champions foreshadowing. These writers and guides insist that, for every twist in a story, there ought to be a foreshadowing line or event.

I just can't get behind that. If you want to foreshadow, go right ahead. But I really don't think you need to. Don't get me wrong. If you are writing a thriller or (especially) a horror story, subtle foreshadowing is a wonderful way to build suspense. Having the hero enter a dark tunnel with just his torch means you *know* something will jump out. The longer he creeps along those corridors, the greater the tension.

But horror also thrives on unexpected jump scares, where you don't see the threat coming. So mix it up. To me, foreshadowing is a handy tool but don't be browbeating into thinking you have to always use it.

Especially when it comes to twists.

Twists

Twists are not the same thing as giving an unexpected answer to a question raised in your story. Twists are surprises the reader doesn't see coming. Sometimes they can be foreshadowed (see **It Was a Dark and Stormy Night**). On other occasions, there are no previous indicators to their imminent presence. To me, they are the magic ingredient in a page-turner and you are the magician. It's about misdirection. Sleight of pen, if you like. Done right, twists fundamentally change your story, shifting it to a new level. A famous example?

Luke. I am your father.

Suddenly, *Star Wars* takes on a depth it never had before. Which is still not very deep, but you take my meaning.

I love a big twist at the end of a story. In *Spiral Wood*, the hero knows her two romantic entanglements are both the same man - something I kept hidden from the reader until the end. When that fact is revealed, all perspectives change and the stakes are so much higher. How do you pick between two sides of the same person? Notice this isn't an original idea - just a romantic application of *Dr Jekyll and Mr Hyde*.

Lead readers along the path your hero is taking, right into an ambush. Make them concentrate on one aspect of the journey before shattering their preconceptions by introducing a piece of essential information you've kept hidden.

In *Hide*, R.D. Slaither is incarcerated for killing his partner, Justin Moore. He tells a detective friend an incredible story (told in flashbacks) about realising Justin is a homicidal maniac who he tried to stop. The reader feels sorry for R.D. and wants him to beat the rap. Then, near the end, a twist comes along. R.D. has held back the identity of the real killer.

The novel is turned on its head. R.D. is no longer the amiable loser he seems but a master manipulator, the detective is his patsy and Justin is innocent. Everything the reader assumes about each character is wrong and, looking back, they see a completely different tale.

A fantastic example is *The Wasp Factory* by Iain Banks. Psychopathic 16-year-old Frank Cauldhame is waiting for the return of his brother, Eric, who has escaped from a psychiatric institution and is batshit crazy. The book is a tense build up (with lots of foreshadowing) to this moment, but that's simply a brilliant MacGuffin. Eric's imminent arrival prompts Frank's father to go get drunk, leaving his study unlocked. And what Frank finds in there changes everything in the most horrible way.

How do you formulate a great twist? Keep an open mind as you write. Use *what if?* in the most bizarre way you can. Look at your plot and think to yourself:

What would really throw a spanner in the works of this well-oiled machine?

Why would you do that? Isn't your story fine as it is? Maybe. Or, perhaps, it could do with a little kick in the pants. Go over your story again and say:

What if this happened? No. No, I couldn't possibly do that. It's insane!

If that's your reaction, it's definitely worth considering. If it astonished you by its boldness, think of what it will do to the reader.

In *Father Figure,* the narrator Donny has a brother called Sam, who committed suicide after his dodgy therapist was sent to jail. Near the end, I suddenly thought:

What if Sam is pretending to be Donny? That he *was the one being treated, and Donny committed suicide because he couldn't cope with looking after his mad brother?*

My first reaction was *nah. I can't do that!* Swiftly followed by *I have to!*

Donny suddenly becomes an unreliable narrator and everything in the book changes, because we don't trust him anymore. The revelation destroys his carefully constructed fake world - an emotional domino run that makes the novel far more powerful.

You'd be surprised how easy a twist, one that comes to you unexpectedly, is to navigate. It doesn't necessarily require huge changes to the plot. It's just a fork in the journey that you didn't see approaching. You just need to go back and make some adjustments so it fits in with what's gone before - or you risk rupturing internal logic (we'll come to that in a second).

First, let's look at the mini twist.

The Mini Twist

The big twist turns a story on its head and often comes near the end. The mini twist serves the same function but is more contained. A controlled explosion rather than a major detonation. Think of it like this.

You have a piece of information that is going to cause a real jolt in the reader's perception of how the story is progressing. Don't just chuck that info in. Sit on it until it will have maximum effect.

In *Waiting For a Train that Never Comes,* 15-year-old Bobby Berlin is fleeing across an empty countryside with his father, Gordon. Gordon has lost his memory and believes he is also a 15-year-old. The big twist at the end is that the countryside is deserted because a tidal wave is coming. The mini twist, however, comes halfway through. It's the discovery that Gordon has forgotten he is supposed to take antipsychotic medication. When that piece of information is revealed, the reader realises this man will slowly become a real threat to his son. Boom! The tension level suddenly shoots up.

The Random Element

I've just talked about surprising yourself and I'm not done with that idea quite yet. In fact, I want to expand on it.

Nuts and bolts are great but a writer wants to be unique. Innovative. Which means thinking outside the box. You can't teach that. However, if there's one practical tip that will lead you in the right direction, it's this one. I guarantee it will give you an advantage over other writers.

Incorporate what is around you. Continuously.

Watch the news. Read interesting articles. Keep your ears open to gossip. Chat to taxi drivers. Ian Rankin of *Inspector Rebus* fame sits in the Oxford Bar in Edinburgh and writes down snippets of conversation to use in his novels. I used to hang around sometimes, hoping he'd hear my pearls of wisdom. He mostly ignored me.

Anyway, that's small potatoes compared to what I'm proposing. I want you to be truly ambitious with the random element.

Look around and take note of arbitrary objects. Pictures on walls. What you find in a side street. Adverts on TV or YouTube and TikTok. Anything. Absolutely anything.

If anything you hear, see or experience grabs your attention, consider incorporating it into your story. I don't mean in a superficial way. I mean, make it integral to the plot, even if it derails your carefully thought-out, existing plan.

Let me return to *Waiting for A Train That Never Comes*. I was fairly sure where it was going. As I've said several times now, it's about a man who wakes up convinced he's a 15-year-old boy with police looking for him. So, he goes on the run, cross country, with his real 15-year-old son. It was coming along nicely when I saw footage of a Tsunami on the news and a huge *what if* suddenly came to me.

What if the countryside was deserted because a tidal wave was coming and this pair were the only two who didn't know? After all, they've ditched their mobiles for fear of being traced.

I couldn't resist it. The plot veered off on a completely different tangent. That random element made for a twist the reader really didn't see coming - because I hadn't. I'd broken into my own story with something completely arbitrary, which immediately became essential. Again I say, if you can surprise yourself, readers will be dumbfounded. A tidal wave? Where the hell did that idea come from?

Things flowed from there, excuse the pun. Evacuated farms and villages in an empty countryside brought a truly sinister aura to the story and made the book much more evocative. It was also a convenient foreshadowing of the disaster to come.

See, I do use it when I've a mind to.

That's the beauty of incorporating something random. It's random. Your readers will never guess what's coming because you didn't. It really is a neat trick and can be used in multiple ways.

In the same book, I wanted my hero to come from a small, boring village. So my girlfriend suggested I call it after a tiny place near her house called Puddledub. No, I'm not making the name up.

I took a look and found there was nothing but a few houses, an old church, a boarding kennel and, in the distance, an ethylene production plant.

All I needed for my book was the name and a few houses but, on impulse, decided to include everything. Not only that, I'd make them all pertinent to the plot. In the process, the ethylene plant became a major player. To make that (and the tidal wave) work, I had to slot in gipsies, an old woman with dementia, a boat smuggling stolen artefacts and a corrupt drilling company and a character with a mysterious hatred of religion.

This trick will work with absolutely everything. Character (use that mad woman you saw chasing a shelf stacker around the supermarket). Description. That's a no-brainer. Dialogue. (Quentin Tarantino does it, I'm positive). *Everything.*

In creating a page-turner, nothing is off the table.

It's your story, and I can only give examples of how I surprised myself. Incorporating random elements into a half-written book meant a bit of hair pulling and a lot of alcohol. In the end, though, it was a lot simpler than I thought.

All I did was overcome the obstacles.

Internal Logic

I'm familiar with the fact that you are going to ignore this particular problem until it swims up and bites you in the ass!

Carl Gottlieb *(Jaws)*

When it comes to entertainment, people will buy into any ridiculous premise. Vampires exist. Vampires are interesting. Vampires are sexy.

Bunker Ten features time travel. Obviously, I've never time travelled unless you count the night I took too many magic mushrooms on Kirriemuir Hill - and that was probably my imagination. I wrote about it anyway and wanted to sound plausible, so I invented the scientific method by which it was possible - stripped light. It might be scientifically unprovable but sounded good and had believable internal logic.

Your killer idea can be so out there you need a telescope to see it and it will make no difference. In fact, many a story has revolved around the protagonist trying to convince people that something weird really is going on. *Invasion of the Body Snatchers* and *Jaws* spring to mind (though *Jaws* is inspired by a real incident). Anything goes, really.

Except when it comes to internal logic. This is something even experienced writers get wrong or ignore until it bites them on the ass.

Jaws is an awesome story, in my opinion (even if the film is far better than the book and much of it is pinched from *Moby Dick*). Plus, its internal logic works decently enough. *Jaws 4: The Revenge*, on the other hand, has a great white shark cross an ocean to get revenge on the widow of Chief Brody from film one.

Where do I begin? The original shark was killed. So an entirely different shark goes hunting for Brody's wife? *What*? How does it find her? How does it even know she was married to Brody? My five-year-old pointed those bloopers out, though she shouldn't actually have been watching either film.

If you've committed yourself to a crazy idea, go for it. But the mechanism of that idea has to work within its own parameters. Internal logic must prevail.

This is exasperating stuff, but you can't be slothful about it. You will come to a point where you look back on what you've written and slap your forehead like they do in cartoons.

Oh crap. Why didn't she just call her brother at this point? He could have cleared the whole thing up.

Don't presume the readers won't notice. You did. It's astonishing how many stories fail the logic test because everything could be cleared up by one text message.

So... you make the hero lose their phone, only to realise they need to use it a few scenes later. No reception, then, even though that's a massive cliché. But they're in the middle of New York City. Damn!

Keep working at it. It'll come. Fixing internal logic or plot flaws often means returning to the beginning and slotting in clues. This, in turn, may open an avenue to go in a more exciting direction. You should always be on the lookout for that chance anyway.

Internal logic applies to characters too. A timid sidekick isn't going to go into that dark tunnel unless you give him a good reason. He might if the brave, bold hero has claustrophobia and the sidekick is desperate to impress a girl. Which, happily, is more surprising and dramatically satisfying than the hero doing it.

I've now laid out suggestions for developing the central idea, plot, beginning and mechanics of your story. The generalities. Now we move on to specifics and the next of the Fab 4. The words you use and the way you use them.

Prose.

Prose

You've written your beginning and are either rolling out your pre-planned plot or struggling along an uncertain path to your destination.

Time to get technical.

Even more than plot, prose can be radically and endlessly altered. Unlike plot, you can leave it all until the story is finished. You don't want to wait that long, though. Why would you?

There are aspects of prose you can fix perfectly well in the revision stage and I'll list them later. Right now, I'm going to mention a couple of related concepts professional writers bandy about while waving their hands theatrically. None of them, I would argue, are as useful as they first appear.

Imagery

> *What I take from writers I like is their economy... for somebody to paint an entire landscape of visual imagery with just sheets of words - that's magical.*

Mos Def

Imagery is using evocative language to create a sharp mental picture. Producing visualisations the reader can't get out of their minds. In theory, anyhow.

Don't go over the score, I beg you. If your story is laden with imagery, no matter how evocative, it slows everything down. Throw in a nice descriptive turn of phrase now and then. That will do the trick.

Voice

Don't try to guess what it is people want and give it to them. Don't ask for a show of hands. Try your best to write what you like, what you think your friends would like and what you think your father would like and then cross your fingers... The most valuable thing you have is your own voice.

Aaron Sorkin

Voice is a hard concept to describe and harder to get right. Just be yourself and don't worry too much about it. Avoid artifice. Try not to copy other writers. Don't be 'arty' because you think it will win you a prize. If your characters are vivid and the dialogue sparkles, that's all you really need.

Some authors write for a market, try to anticipate trends or follow a template.

Couple meet + they fall in love – something gets in the way + they overcome it = successful romance.

Fact is, you'll never become the writer you want to be unless you do you. Your 'voice' will evolve naturally - it comes with experience and getting to know your own mind. My writing has changed a great deal over 20 years but, for better or worse, it remains mine. I try new things, keep what I like and ditch the rest.

Understand that, while imagery and voice are integral to the process of writing a good story, 'integration' is the key word. Concentrate on the Fab 4 - plot, prose, character and dialogue. Get those right and other aspects will kind of... well... integrate themselves.

Exclamation marks

F. Scott Fitzgerald said *an exclamation point is like laughing at your own joke*.

They're OK for arguments, attacks and warnings but cheesy everywhere else. In narration, they are strident and make everything seem shouty. Unless a character is actually yelling, try not to use them.

All caps are even worse. CUT THEM OUT!

Adjectives

Most adjectives are unnecessary. Like adverbs, they are sprinkled into sentences by writers who don't stop to think that the concept is already in the noun.

William Zinsser:

Adjectives are words naming an attribute of a noun, such as *sweet* or *red*.

Writers love adjectives. They add colour and body to sentences. And everyone uses them too often. Overuse makes sentences drag and, in my view, is talking down to the audience. Full, ruby-red, luscious, wet lips? That's taking things way too far. Your reader knows what lips look like. I'll dwell on this more when I come to **Description**.

In the meantime, the best lesson I can think of comes from the incomparable C. S. Lewis.

Don't use adjectives which merely tell us how you want us to feel about the thing you are describing. I mean, instead of telling us a thing was "terrible," describe it so that we'll be terrified. Don't say it was "delightful"; make us say "delightful" when we've read the description. You see, all those words (horrifying, wonderful, hideous, exquisite) are only like saying to your readers, "Please will you do my job for me."

Adverbs

Substitute 'damn' every time you're inclined to write 'very;' your editor will delete it and the writing will be just as it should be.

Mark Twain

Adverbs are words that modify verbs, adjectives and other adverbs.

He drove a very fast car. It moved quite quickly down the mountainside.

Everything I've said about adjectives goes for adverbs too. Always look to be cutting superfluous ones. In the above examples, *quite* and *very* can go without changing the sentence one tiny, little, minuscule bit.

Similes

A simile is a figure of speech involving the comparison of one thing with another thing of a different kind, used to make a description more emphatic or vivid.

Brave as a lion.

A good simile is like a breath of fresh air (see what I did there?). That was a bad simile because it is also a cliché. A bad simile sticks out like a sore thumb (also a cliché).

Good authors keep similes to a minimum and only put them in when a really awesome one occurs. The comedian Steve Martin captured this perfectly when he said: *A day without sunshine is like, y'know, night.*

Avoid clichés but also avoid coming up with similes that are ridiculous in their quest for originality unless you are writing a farce.

She had a deep, throaty, genuine laugh, like that sound a dog makes just before it throws up.

Metaphors

A metaphor is a figure of speech that describes an object or action in a way that isn't literally true but helps explain an idea or make a comparison. It can be used in two ways. The first is a metaphorical action.

My heart leapt into my mouth.

Sounds painful. Unfortunately, this is also a cliché and should be avoided. It's almost impossible to write something that nobody has written before so, if you must use a metaphorical cliché, keep it short. Don't draw attention to it.

My heart leapt is not nearly so bad.

Metaphors are also used to state that one thing *is* another thing.

Love is a battlefield.

This is also a cliché.

The same rules apply to metaphors as they do to similes. Go too far in your quest for originality and you'll write something daft. Similes and metaphors are minefields, waiting to blow up a paragraph like an atomic bomb.

See what I did there?

Analogies.

Yeah. I'm not even going to go there.

Expletives

Fuck no! Not those kinds of expletives. Expletives are words or phrases used to pad out a sentence without changing its meaning. They are sometimes referred to as empty words. The key word here is pad. In other words, you don't need them.

The following is from the book *Storycraft* by the journalist Jack Hart. I could paraphrase, but if you want clear advice on prose, ask a journalist - so I may as well go straight to the source.

Any word that doesn't advance a story slows it down. Which is reason enough to avoid expletives. Contrary to popular misconception, the term "expletive" refers to a whole class of empty words, not just gratuitous profanities. Most expletives simply fill out the syntax of sentences. The most common are 'there are', 'there is', 'there was', 'it is', 'it was', and so on.

Think about a sentence like 'there were two airplanes on the runway'. What's the 'there' refer to, anyway? Nada. It just serves to turn 'two airplanes on the runway' into a complete sentence.

You don't violate any grammatical rule when you use an expletive, and each expletive is of no great consequence. But they pile up, and eventually they slow your storytelling.

Why not introduce a real verb that generates an image by writing 'two airplanes taxied on the runway' or 'two airplanes idled on the runway', or even 'two airplanes sat on the runway'?

Getting all these techniques right will improve the quality of your writing and you've probably seen an overall guideline emerging. It is absolutely essential and can be summed up in three words.

Less is more.

Less is more applies even more to the next section. It covers the part of prose many writers approach with gung-ho enthusiasm and a misplaced determinism to show how well they can write - not realising this will be their undoing.

Description.

Description

One day I will find the right words, and they will be simple.

Jack Kerouac

You Don't Need Five Pages to Describe a Horse

I'm not kidding about the horse. OK, it may not have been exactly five pages but it certainly seemed like it by the time I stopped reading and threw the book across the room. I forget the name of the story. I know it won a major prize.

If you fancy writing a literary masterpiece that will win the *Worthy But Hard to Read* award, load up your novel with masses of descriptions. I'm trying to help you craft a page-turner. I know what a horse looks like and so does the reader. *It was big and brown with a vile temperament* will do nicely.

The writer Dan Brown says:

Lead your reader from point to point. Their imagination will fill in the blanks.

An audience is quite capable of forming a picture in their heads of where your hero happens to be. Or how he feels. If he's running for his life and his breath is coming in terrified spurts, they will deduce his state of mind pretty easily. You don't even have to dwell on what he looks like. My heroes are perfunctorily described. Short and wiry with sandy hair. Tall with red hair and freckles. Stout, with a gap between her front teeth. Unless you're writing about the *Elephant Man*, readers can envisage the rest.

Don't be Flowery
Dean Koontz is a master of the page-turner and has sold 450 million books, so I'm not going to sneeze at his advice.

There is one rule of style that every writer can benefit from: say it as simply, as clearly, and as shortly as possible. Only two genres are hospitable to the baroque style of writing - fantasy and Gothic-romance; all other categories are better suited to crisp, lean prose.

Baroque writing, incidentally, is characterised by the use of figurative language such as similes and metaphors - as well as other literary devices like hyperbole and imagery. In other words, flowery.

Getting overly florid in your descriptions is a common trap. Being able to describe something beautifully is an art and you may be tempted to show how good you are at it. But being able to describe something beautifully in one sentence is also an art - and that's what you should be aiming for. Want to see a masterful, one sentence, go for the jugular, portrayal? This is from *The Great Gatsby* by F. Scott Fitzgerald.

If personality is an unbroken series of successful gestures, then there was something gorgeous about him.

Boom! He nails the guy, just like that. Without the slightest bit of normal description, he portrays a man who is enviable on the surface yet somehow sad and empty beneath. Even if he does use an empty expletive by keeping in the word *then*.

Or take this opening line from *A Letter to Julia* by Isabel Clemente.

Around the fire, on cold winter nights, we played with the flight of sparks hoping they would join the stars.

At first glance, it looks descriptive. Only, it's not, is it? She doesn't describe the fire or the night or the stars or the sparks. She mentions them in a way that creates a powerful image. Though not strictly accurate, I'd call this more of a depiction. If description is providing information, depiction is giving a visual representation. If description is *tell*, depiction is *show*.

Less is more. Don't describe. Depict.

As I've said before, writing speculative fiction means you may have built a whole world you want the reader to get lost in. Naturally, that requires a proper depiction and you shouldn't skimp. Just remember you need original ideas more than lots of detail. Beautiful representations won't hide a realm filled with boring people or recycled from parts of other books.

If you want a jaw-dropping example of originality, read *On* by Adam Roberts. Set on a giant wall, the setting is impeccably and nightmarishly thought up and rendered, with an incredible twist. The wall generates its own obstacles and inspires utterly original ones. Tellingly, I think things rather fall apart when the description starts to become too long and technical.

I've already gone into world building in the **Settings** section but some advice bears repeating. Even if your story is set in a fascinating time or incredible location, don't go overboard portraying it. Rather than using long sentences, intersperse short depictions throughout your scenes. Venice has a lot of canals. You only need to describe one properly. The Grand Canal is much bigger than the others. There are gondolas everywhere. It smells in summer.

Let necessity guide you. In *The Armageddon Twins,* the protagonists hide out at a house in the country. It's set back from the main road behind a high wall. It has a wooden balcony. There's a big oak outside with a tree house, high in the branches. An old-fashioned stone fireplace with a working chimney. An abandoned tractor in the field next door. A basement workshop with a hidden trapdoor in the cupboard. A computer and wall map in the study. Only one door in and out of the building. Large plate-glass windows with no lattices.

All these are included because they are integral to the plot or the action when it breaks out. But what I've just stated was pretty much all readers were given. Most were only introduced when needed and I added in a couple more descriptive phrases as each came into play.

If you won't encounter or need it later, don't bother describing it.

If you are overcome by the need to portray something at length, don't do so in the middle of an action or dramatic scene. Get rid of adjectives and adverbs. Tone down metaphors and similes. Streamline all descriptions.

Less is more.

Read what you've written out loud. Is that the way you'd tell it to your friends if you were recounting a real event? If they begin to fidget, or you feel you're not getting to the point, it's too verbose.

Good description is about the pinpoint sharp image, not a great wordy canvas. The writer Richard Price states it perfectly.

The bigger the issue the smaller you write. You don't write about the horrors of war. No. You write about a kid's burnt socks lying in the road. You pick the smallest manageable part of the big thing, and you work off the resonance.

Overacting

Excessive verbosity and flowery prose create a quagmire the reader will not relish wading through. However, there's another, more subtle kind of overwriting, which I'm going to call 'overacting'. This is not about describing things as expansively as possible but putting in lots of irrelevant details for the sake of it.

These tend to be small actions that are completely reasonable and not needed at all. The equivalent of someone trying to tell you a fun story but including the fact that it took place on a Tuesday, which part of the street it occurred and whether the sun was shining or not.

I've said it before and I'll say it again. If you're telling a story to your friends, you should breeze through it and stick to the entertaining parts. Writing it down is no different.

A picture may paint a thousand words but it doesn't take a thousand words to paint a picture.

Trust your reader's imagination. Keep your prose lean and clean.

Less is more.

Show Don't Tell II

I've already mentioned *show don't tell* but I want to reinforce that advice. If you are presenting the reader with a picture, don't just point to it on the wall. Let them see you paint it.

What kind of things can we do to illustrate that poorly conceived analogy? Here's one example.

Your descriptions will work better if they are interactive rather than narrative.

Rather than relating a slab of info, the reader's experience of the story's setting can best be seen through the prism of the characters.

When I go into my kitchen, how do I describe it? I usually check out what food is lying around. I gaze lovingly at my big shiny fridge and collection of magnets and mugs from around the world. This shows I love to travel and I'm a greedy pig who loves ceramic tat.

When my partner enters her kitchen, she immediately focuses on the crumbs, dirty dishes and footwear scattered across the floor. It makes her want to get out the Hoover and shout at me.

Same room, two different interpretations. What's more, the descriptions tell you about these characters and can even drive the plot.

Talking of driving the plot. While excessive description is a no-no, so is trying to get around it by putting awkward words in your character's mouths.

Oh, my God. There's a glowing green figure in the doorway!

This is not something a real person would say. *What the hell is that?* is better. Then briefly describe what the character is looking at. Briefly.

Only if nobody else has seen this apparition, or you don't want the reader to know whether it's real or not, should the character elaborate.

Exceptions

No purple prose or overacting. I've stated it like a rule but it's more of a strong suggestion. And, as with all writing rules or suggestions, there are exceptions.

Sometimes you want to cut loose with description. It's irresistible. What's more, it occasionally enhances a story. I wracked my brains and this is the most descriptive passage I can think of that I've written - from my novel *Hide*.

It follows a scene of intense action and (if you remember the **Pace and Tension** section) it was time to slow things down. I wanted to create a sense of sadness, unease and menace without stating it directly. Therefore, I used more description than I usually would. I borrowed the bleak imagery of film noir and horror and kept dialogue to a minimum.

The description was *designed* to slow everything down. To create a calm before the storm. A period of contemplation and reflection. To let it sink in that our hero is about to lose everything and, what's more, is beginning to realise it.

Before long, a set of boxy Aluminium bunkhouses oozed over the horizon. The bulb rimmed sign on top of the largest proudly proclaimed Southern Star Motel. *Underneath a plastic slot-in board cheerfully added* The Schneiders Welcome You. Rooms from $25.00. *On tatty porches empty concrete flowerpots guarded identical school green doors. Mosquitoes hovered above each foot-high container, pickled in luminescence, flowers without stems.*

"May as well stop here, eh?" R.D. spun into the driveway. "It's a shithole, so the tone will be in keeping with the rest of the day."

He glanced at Maggie's miserable, hunched form.

"I don't care if Norman Bates owns the damned place." The woman wearily reached for her purse. "So long as it's got the shower as well."

They were given a double at the back of the motel, which boasted a sterling view of a partly constructed truck stop. Off to the left, the tarmac and lights ended abruptly in one monster sized bite, a cavity littered with workmen's tools, looking like they'd been dropped in flight. To the right, construction had been finished and several low rigs huddled round the safety of illuminated gas pumps.

Now that he could sleep, R.D. didn't mind delaying the moment. Leaving Maggie to freshen up he floundered across the masticated earth to the service station, bought a 12-pack, soldiered back and settled into a plastic deck chair. Planting his feet on the porch rail, he opened an Old Milwaukee, lit a cigarette and puffed out an orbit of smoke to keep the multiformed bugs away.

The door behind him opened and Maggie stepped out to cool down after her shower. For a while neither of them spoke. R.D. chugged the beer and his escort let the night breezes dry her dark hair. The scent of cheap motel soap blended with cigarette smoke, then fainter diesel fumes on the other side of the highway.

Over there, trucks croaked like bullfrogs in their floodlit pond, a husky lullaby of throttles opening and closing. Chrome mammoths woke and slumbered, pulling themselves on and off the freeway. Every so often, a truck door slammed and a snatch of Country and Western music wafted up to the porch.

R.D. twisted to look at his companion. Her face was mostly shadow but the oil-black narrow eyes were glistening.

"Nice place you got here," she whispered.

Had she been crying? R.D. couldn't tell. Maggie's hands were laced behind her body and she leant casually against the door frame, staring over the gas station to a sky damp with stars. Though her hair had begun to dry, lightening and curling around her face, the water from washing still darkened the front of her dress. Shapely smooth legs curved over each other, glistening with moonlight mottled moisture.

Standing there, she looked more like a femme fatale than a tired, frightened girl - a powerful monochrome marriage of practicality and dread. This was probably the most beautiful Maggie Wood was ever going to get. And R.D. had to admit, it was close to perfect.

Note that I also broke my own instructions about showing what characters think and feel. Every rule has exceptions and this was one.

Exercise 4

Take a chapter from a wordy old-fashioned novel like Moby Dick. *Write it in the modern vernacular.*

Conjuring up Characters

Settings are obviously important... But the real key to success lies in finding the right characters.

Joan Lingard

When writing a novel a writer should create living people; people not characters. A character is a caricature.

Ernest Hemingway

There you go. Hemmingway and Lingard apparently contradicting each other on characters. Here's what they do agree on, though. They are the key to a great story.

Plot, prose, character and dialogue. The Fab 4.

You may have a fair idea of what your heroes are like before you begin but it's not strictly necessary. Until I introduce a person on the page, even a main character, I've no idea of their personality. Like the reader, I will find that out as I go along.

What can I say? I like surprises.

You Are a Little God

I've said I find out a character's personality as I go along. That's a little disingenuous. Writers wax lyrical about 'falling in love' with their own characters, as if they were real. They decree you need to know them inside out and that the story develops from how they interact with the world.

I bloody hope you know them inside out. You made them. I have a great fondness for many of my characters and relate to them better than my own friends. But I don't forget that they are made up and the most important relationship they can have is with the reader. Nor do your characters drive the plot. That's an illusion. You do.

You are the creator of your stories and you call the shots.

While it's important to remember your characters do not really have autonomy, you want to treat them *as if* they do. If your protagonists are well-defined, you and your audience know how they will act and what they will or won't do. If the reader experiences a character as a real person, they will be more invested in their journey and arc.

That's why grey areas are so satisfying. When your protagonist faces the impossible choice - or a dramatic situation where their decision could go either way - the stakes are so much higher.

Remember Nagel? In real life, we can never really know anyone. However much authors may protest, on the other hand, we *do* know our characters and how they will react in any given situation. Because we created them.

But the *reader* doesn't and it's often better that way. Even if you choose to let them in on a character's thoughts, the reader can never be sure they are not dealing with human foibles or an unreliable narrator.

It's quantum mechanics again. The observer affects the outcome of what is being observed. As with encountering a real person, readers observe what is being said and what is going on. Then they use those observations to decide what kind of person the character is. If you've crafted a convincing protagonist, they'll happily keep reading to find out if they are right. That's what makes a page-turner.

It's a neat dichotomy. Like a little God, you control every single aspect of your story, including the characters' thoughts, feelings and actions. The trick is to make it look like the exact opposite. You're not a merciful God, either. You're going to test your creations and make them suffer.

I'll be blunt. Given the breadth of human variety, it's virtually impossible to create a character who isn't realistic. No matter how strange a proclivity may seem to you, somebody has done it. The movie *Jumbo* is about a woman who falls in love with a fairground attraction. Wow. Only, it's based on a real phenomenon, Objectum Sexuality or Objectophilia, which has seen one woman marry the Eiffel Tower and another a bridge.

That's going to be a little too weird for most romance readers, though it's a great film. On the other side of the scale, a dull character is also realistic - since a huge number of human beings are rather boring. The same goes for people who are petty, vindictive, ignorant, populist, racist, homophobic and transphobic.

Problem is, they're not people you want to read about unless they do a complete about-face by the end of the book – which is not particularly realistic.

So, what's the best way to get yourself characters the reader is going to want to follow?

Make the Reader Care

The readers don't have to like your protagonist but they do have to care about them. Often the two go hand in hand. They'll like *and* care about a character who is kind and decent and stands up to bullies. A hero who is Peter Perfect will often turn out bland, so make sure they have flaws, like a real person. Readers will care as much about a damaged character as an ideal one - if they have at least one of the following traits.

Make Them Funny.

I'm not talking about comic relief or a court jester type. Simply people who come out with a neat line now and then. Just make sure it's in keeping with their character. A deeply flawed person is just as capable of bringing the yuks as a saint. Probably more so. While someone with a droll sense of humour isn't going to break into an over-the-top cabaret routine. Most people occasionally say something witty. If they don't, why would you want to hang out with them?

Characters are the same. (See **Dialogue**) .

Make Them the Underdog

No surer way to get the reader on the protagonist's side than pitting them against overwhelming odds.

It's why I dislike superheroes. Any problems they have seem irrelevant to me. Can't reveal your secret identity? Get over yourself. You can fly.

Have Them Overcome their Own Flaws

Everyone has flaws of one sort or another. Me more than most. Give your main characters weaknesses that make it all the more difficult to overcome the obstacles they face. If the obstacles arise *because* of their flaws, so much the better. Then they have to get right and sort themselves out if they want a happy ever after.

Start with the general and move on to specifics.

Don't go crazy with flaws, though. Your reader will sympathise with a recovering alcoholic. A recovering serial killer is going to have to be hella funny before the reader gets on board.

Have Them Do 'The Thing'

Your character is a despicable nurk. Then they do 'the thing'. While running from danger, they stop to pick up a cat. They cry at a wedding. They switch sides in battle. They show off their snow globe collection.

Readers love to see a crack in the armour.

Get Dickensian

Here's another observation that is often frowned upon but I like.

Make your central character under-formed.

If you do this, the reader can project themselves onto them. In *Oliver Twist* by Charles Dickens, Oliver is a nondescript nobody. It's the villains - Bill Sykes, the Artful Dodger, Fagan and Nancy - who make the book. That's who Dickens was interested in. His 'hero' is little more than a plot device to ensure we get plenty of them.

There are also a couple of traits that some writers seem to think make their characters endearing but really don't. Be very careful when messing about with these two.

At Least I'm Good at my Job

There is a curious conception that we will care about a character simply because they are good at what they do. I.e. warriors, hitmen and soldiers. This is not true outside the USA. If you are a corporate lawyer, for instance, your likability factor is actually in inverse proportion to how well you do your job. The character has to have bags of charisma or be conflicted about what they do for the reader to care.

Hi. I'm Handsome

This is a trap many a romance writer falls into. Looking good is not a character trait any more than being tall is. It's simply a description. You can make an dickwad handsome but he'll still be a dickwad.

Don't Get Too Emotional

What your character does reveals who they are. What they say reveals who they see themselves as.

Aaron Sorkin

I'm going to repeat myself again with the *show don't tell* advice. You are a little God, so you *can* allow the reader to know exactly what your protagonists are thinking and feeling. Again, I urge you to be sparing in this department. You are a storyteller, not an analyst.

Make the readers *work* to understand your characters. Don't lay it out for them. Readers *should* be unsure about a character's motivations until they get to know them. And they should get to know them by observing what they say and do, not by some magical insight into their mind. As the writer Hermann Hesse said:

Words do not express thoughts very well. They always become a little different immediately after they are expressed, a little distorted, a little foolish.

That inability to properly express thoughts is natural and forgivable if coming from a character. Not so much if it's coming from a narrator.

If you are telling your friends a story about someone, you don't go tend to go deeply into the motivations and personality of those involved. You simply tell the tale and your pals glean an insight into the subject's traits and reasons from that.

If you write in the first person, it's impossible not to show what the protagonist is thinking and feeling. You may even have more than one first-person character. I'd still advocate toning down emotions and letting words and actions speak louder than thoughts. Don't turn your hero into a moody *Hamlet* type who can't go to the toilet without agonising about it in blank verse.

Once more, with no emotion. When you can, show what characters think by their conversations and interactions. You can even use imagery rather than blatantly pointing out how someone feels.

I'll give an example from an episode of *Primal* I just watched. The entire series has no dialogue or voiceover, making images key to deciphering the characters' mental state.

In one incident, the Viking-style villain returns to his village to find the hero has killed his wife and child. How's *that* for a subversion of the norm? As he places his loved ones into a burning boat, we see the flames reflected in his eyes and know his desire for revenge will never be quenched. All without a word.

One more thing about feelings. Many writers have a tendency to keep their protagonist's emotional dials turned up to eleven, especially in romance and YA stories. Keep that toned down too. Remember pace and tension. Excitement. Relax. Excitement. Relax.

There are only so many times a character can clench their fist or feel their heart pound before the reader gets thoroughly sick of them.

Villains

Every villain has their belief system that makes perfect sense to them.

Patty Jenkins

A huge proportion of page-turners have a hero or heroes who must overcome a villain or villains. It can be the whole plot or just an aspect of it.

In its purest form, it's good versus evil. Which, although it is still done to death, is overly simplistic and doesn't ring true. Narrative and character arcs are about overcoming obstacles. A villain is only one of many possible obstacles.

There's nothing wrong with a boo-hiss outlaw if all you want is pure adventure, horror or comedy. Don't be lazy, though. You don't want a one-dimensional hero, so why settle for a cardboard baddie? The villain can actually think what he's doing is right or, at least, justify his actions. Remember, bad guys are human too - unless they're killer androids. The boring villain as obstacle is no more acceptable than the boring hero.

The labels 'hero' and 'villain' are useful but don't really do a good story justice. In reality, what you have is one character versus another character. If you're clever, the reader won't be entirely sure which side they want to root for. It's always more interesting if a conflict isn't black or white. Film maker David Fincher says:

Make sure that in any argument, everyone is right. I want every single person arguing a righteous side of the argument. That makes interesting drama.

In *The Armageddon Twins,* the heroes are aided by an Artificial Intelligence that manipulates them mercilessly. It's not until near the end that you find out whether it's really on their side. They also recruit a vicious killer to their cause and are never sure if he will turn on them. Uncertainty generates emotional friction and is a great way of ensuring those pages keep getting turned.

Incidentally, the vicious killer doesn't have a character arc where he gets all warm and fuzzy. He has a witty turn of phrase and decides, in the end, to side with the good guys. That's enough to turn him from 'villain' to 'hero'. In reality, he is neither. So what? He makes for a lively read.

In *Waiting For The Train That Never Comes*, one of the main characters believes he is someone else, making him both hero and villain. The struggle for dominance is entirely within himself. The main 'villain' turns out to be a different type of obstacle entirely - a tidal wave. There's no way any of the characters can escape it or beat it, so their journey cannot end in victory. It merely becomes a question of whether they will survive.

Minor Characters

Minor characters should serve a purpose, no matter how oblique. They can be comic relief. Cannon fodder.

A red herring. Someone holding a crucial piece of information which will come out later.

Never give them all internal monologues, as this will make the book sluggish. The ability to show what they think and feel with dialogue and action alone is even more important for a bit player.

In a page-turner, secondary characters are mainly there to advance the story or, at least, flesh it out. If a person is only in one scene, playing a small role, you don't even have to give them a name. Leave out backstories that will kill the pace. Sketch them quickly and make them crisply memorable. There are several tricks for doing this.

Quirky Names

Particularly helpful if you have a large cast and another trick Charles Dickens employed to great effect. I'm not suggesting you call a character Reginald Cornobbler (though I actually have) but don't choose something mundane. *Father Figure* has characters called Daisy Lenin and Donny Marigold. Not outlandish but by no means ordinary.

If they do have a normal moniker, assign them a nickname, especially one that suits their character. This also allows you to alternate their real and nicknames, avoiding repetition. In *Spiral Wood,* Dorothy Arrowsmith is nicknamed Dark, while *Carnage* features teenagers Mondo, Dax and Oakley.

Base Characters on People You Know.

Use their speech patterns, mannerisms, gestures and beliefs. It's the perfect shortcut to creating a realistic human because they *are* a real human. Even being boring is no detriment in a minor character, as long as you intend them to be that way. If not, add a few flourished of your own to spice them up. Make sure you change their name or warn them first, though.

Especially if their character is a bit of an asshole.

Give Them a Unique Way of Speaking.

Do they use a lot of slang? Speak formally? Are they foul-mouthed? Do they use short, clipped sentences or are they verbose?

You don't want to stereotype but be courageous. *Carnage* has a black rapper called Bangles. I trawled through websites of Chicago gangsta slang, printed a glossary, memorized it and watched a heap of movies and rap videos to give the character as authentic a voice as I could manage. It was so much fun, Bangles quickly became a major player.

Publishers hated the idea, saying it was cultural appropriation (see **Appropriation**). I don't deny it but happen to know a couple of black New York ghetto kids (don't ask) and they got behind it. In fact, they gave me pointers. *Carnage* also had two Edinburgh Neds (short for non-educated delinquents). Because I'm Scottish, it was easy to mimic the way they talked and also a delight. So they were promoted to main characters as well. Incidentally, both were based on real kids I met and had no problem with their portrayal either. Their only condition was that, if I used them, they were to die horribly.

I obliged.

Have them Wear a Sombrero

Use one piece of description to make your minor character stand out. A facial tick. A big moustache. A hearing aid. They can be bald or extremely short. Permanently wear a Stetson or a scarf. The more original, the better. And it's always fun if you can reveal something hidden behind an affectation. For example, they may wear a scarf because they're hiding a huge scar around their neck. *Why?* There's that word again. All you have to do is provide an answer that fits the plot further down the line.

Use One Word to Describe Them to Yourself.

Self-obsessed. Melancholy. Sarcastic. Pushy. Earnest. Rude. This will define the character in your head. Then have them act and speak accordingly. Earlier, I mentioned Einstein's quote *God is in the details* was actually coined by the architect Ludwig Mies van der Rohe. A character who points out stuff like that every chance they get, for instance, is a smartass.

Characters become more realistic and exciting, however, if they occasionally break out of that mould. This can be for a number of reasons, like being faced with the impossible choice. Other times it means the character arc has landed and the hero has learned, grown or changed. If internal logic allows, it can even be an extreme change, leading to a cheer out loud moment. Miserly Ebenezer Scrooge's conversion in Charles Dickens' *A Christmas Carol* is a wonderful example.

Personality over Looks.

> *When introducing a character, focus less on physical description and more on their psychological nature and personality. Think in terms of "They're the kind of person who…"*

Christopher Nolan

The cool thing is, all these traits and affectation I've just set out will work for main characters too. Just remember this.

When sketching characters, physical description matters less than personality traits.

Once you've got characters straight in your head, set out their mannerisms, past and inner lives. Nothing complicated. Simply know if they are the kind of person who hates hugging, gets easily embarrassed or cries at sad movies.

In *The Armageddon Twins,* the grumpy hero, Charlie, never smiles and Daffodil has a weird accent nobody can place. In *The Kirkfallen Stopwatch,* the protagonist, Dan Salty, has a sociopathic personality and uses the fact that he will never break a promise as his moral compass. As well as cementing their character, this trick sets up questions. Will Charlie ever smile? Once and it's on the last page. Where is Daffodil's accent from? Watching Westerns on TV. What will it do to Dan Salty if he has to break a promise to the woman he loves? It destroys him.

Your audience will keep reading to find out.

Never have someone act out of character simply to advance the plot. It insults the reader's intelligence and defeats internal logic. You have a knight who is brave and noble, then runs away from a fight? That's great because the reader now wants to know *why*. Give them a reason eventually but make it plausible. If it turns out he took off because he just got his armour back from the dry cleaners, you'll lose trust. Nobody *ever* goes into a creepy basement with a torch but no weapon if there's a serial killer on the loose. Might be good for tension but doesn't ring true.

A Cast of Thousands

Fellow editors sometimes complain about stories with too many characters. Being Scottish, I know an easy solution to this. Pretend you're making a low budget film or play and you have to personally pay for the actors. You'll soon figure out who isn't necessary. It's easy to amalgamate characters, cutting down on confusion while providing the same information.

Personally, I love a cast of thousands. What these editors are really saying is that the cast isn't portrayed particularly well. Fortunately, it's an easy fix.

Treat a big cast the same way as you would flashbacks or tense changes. It's unlikely they will all be together all the time. So whenever you switch from one group to another, make it a new section or paragraph.

If you do have characters together, make sure you don't head hop. This is where the writer switches points of view without warning, often in the same paragraph. It's confusing for the reader to think they are reading one person's thoughts, only to realize they have jumped into the head of somebody else.

Again, treat a change in POV like switching groups. Start a new scene or chapter. Even a line gap will do. Just keep in mind that the more perspectives you have, the easier it is to get everything snarled up. And, if you're writing a romance, using alternating POV's of the lovers has been done to death.

If you have a lot of protagonists, it really does behove you to treat them like minor characters and use the methods I've just suggested - at least initially.

In *Carnage,* I had fifteen main characters fighting for survival and needed to quickly set them apart. That fight was also a great catalyst for a character arc, where the characters found themselves in situations forcing them to act in a way they normally wouldn't.

Siobhan is a self-obsessed vlogger but her obsession turns toward revealing the truth at any cost. Tyler and Ryan are petty thieves turned knights in armour. (I used symbolism to stress this - they literally don suits of armour). Mondo is the cool kid who crumbles under pressure. Dax is a loner reluctantly assuming the mantle of leadership. Andrew is a public schoolboy who condescends to gay Korean Man-Bok until they form an unshakeable bond. Sammy is a quiet scholar who falls in love with Bangles, a streetwise ghetto kid.

Appropriation

This is a massively thorny subject but I guess it has to be covered. So here's my take.

If you're a middle-aged white man like me, it doesn't stop you writing about a young black woman. You can even tell your story from her point of view, say dealing with prejudice in 1930s Alabama.

You *can* do it but I'm not sure why you would.

Being terrified is a universal feeling. If you are a white man in Australia, living in constant fear because of your skin colour is not. I've been ostracised, faced prejudice and been threatened by a nutter with a gun. Yet I've never experienced anything remotely like what that character would face, so I'd be reluctant to make her plight central to any story I write.

That doesn't mean shying away completely. If you are writing a thriller set in 1930s Alabama, you'd be glossing over history if you didn't mention racism and prejudice.

Plus, your job is to use imagination. *Father Figure* has a romance between a compulsive fantasist and a girl with learning difficulties. Obviously, I'm neither. I was once diagnosed as having a sociopathic personality but that's another story. Point is, I can't have all my novels featuring a devastatingly handsome, middle-aged white male named Jan.

Appropriation means you can pay a heavy price with agents and publishers. *Burnt Out* has a recently invalided and suicidal wheelchair user trapped in a burning tower block. The obstacles were obvious and so was the universal theme. How the presence of terrible danger can make you realise how much you want to live.

I have no idea what it's like to be disabled and I'll never get into the mindset of not being able to walk. The best I could do was send the book to wheelchair users. Fortunately, they responded positively.

Then my agent told me I couldn't have a disabled person be suicidal, as it wasn't portraying them in a positive light. This claim prompted a barrage of disbelief from disabled people I talked to. *Everyone* can feel suicidal. I stuck to my guns.

In the end, the arguments were irrelevant. Publishers wouldn't touch *Burn Out* because the Grenfell fire happened just as I finished writing it.

'Appropriation' is a minefield with excellent arguments against creating characters way outside your cultural, mental or physical experience. Especially when it shuts out minorities who are better placed to tell those stories. However, I believe that should be a stick to beat rapacious publishers with, rather than a moral dispute.

If I have to pick a side, I tend towards allowing creativity to take you wherever you want. Just don't be a dick about it. Get advice from the people who fall into the categories you don't really understand and respect what they say. You may not be best placed to directly tell their stories but you can include them in yours.

Nor is culture an exclusive club. I believe other societies and groups should be accessible to those who want to understand or embrace them. 'Otherness' is never something we should avoid.

I was not born in Scotland and my parents are not Scottish. But *I* am. And, being Scottish, I will fight anyone who says I can't be. So here's my final tip.

Do not mistake cultural appreciation for cultural appropriation.

Pitfalls

Lastly, here are a couple of bits of popular character advice I'm not too keen on. You may love them. I'm just putting it out there.

Some books will tell you to understand your character by following these guidelines.

What is their goal? What is their motivation? What happens if they don't achieve their goal?

This is only helpful to a point. What if your character's goal is to stay home and watch Netflix? It's a rubbish motivation but you can still have a great story if he has to fight off a criminal organisation first, then romance the neighbour cause his TV got broken in the battle and he wants to watch the big game.

There's also an opinion that your character's 'big flaw' will keep preventing them from overcoming obstacles and becoming their best self. By the end of the story, they will beat that flaw and learn an important lesson.

Ah, if only life was really like that. We all have flaws. We don't all overcome them.

We just need to conquer the other obstacles.

Exercise 5

Take your favourite character and describe them in three words.

Find a scene you love from your favourite movie or book. Now take out the hero of the scene and replace them with your character. Write the scene and see how it plays out with your new protagonist.

As well as being fun, this is an exercise you can repeat with lots of your characters in lots of other scenes.

Dialogue

Dialogue is not just quotation. It is grimaces, pauses, adjustments of blouse buttons, doodles on a napkin, and crossings of legs.

Jerome Stern

Dialogue trumps everything.

Good characters bring your novel to life. Good dialogue brings the characters to life. Get it right, and the reader will forgive many other shortcomings in your story.

When Andrew Davies began modifying Jane Austin's *Pride and Prejudice* for TV, he stated that he hardly needed to adapt the text at all. Much of the background and setting were already conveyed through conversations between the Bennets.

Dialogue tells you more than first meets the eye. Sticking with excellent old romances, check out this well-known conversation between Jane and Rochester from Charlotte Brontë's *Jane Eyre*.

144 · Let's Write a Page Turner!

"It would please me now to draw you out and learn more of you - therefore speak."

Instead of speaking, I smiled; and not a very complacent or submissive smile either.

"Speak," he urged.

"About what, sir?"

"Whatever you like. I leave both the choice of subject and the manner of treating it entirely to yourself."

Accordingly, I sat and said nothing.

Apart from the content of the conversation, what else does the dialogue tell us? The setting is Victorian England and there's a power struggle going on between two strong but very different personalities. Rochester is blunt, while Jane is subtle. Rochester's attitude and pushiness shows he has higher status than Jane. He fancies her but is highly uncomfortable being intimate, resorting to bluster. What Jane says is polite enough but she's quietly rebellious and much more in charge of the situation. Her silence at the end only reinforces that.

Dialogue is about what remains unsaid as well as what is voiced. Playwright Anita Sullivan cites Cormac McCarthy's *The Road* as an example. Moving through an apocalyptic landscape where survivors fight for resources, father and son have this conversation.

In the floor of this room was a door or hatch and it was locked with a large padlock of stacked steel plates. He stood looking at it.

Papa, the boy said. We should go. Papa.

There's a reason this is locked.

The boy pulled at his hand. He was almost in tears. Papa? he said.

We've got to eat.

I'm not hungry, Papa. I'm not.

Prose and dialogue are stripped to essentials with no indication of emotion. Gotta love that. Yet the sense they are arguing about a life-or-death decision supercharges every word.

The boy pulled at his hand tells you how urgent the child's voice sounds and we know he's lying about not being hungry because he denies it twice. Me? I'd even get rid of the line *He was almost in tears.* His fear and despair are obvious without it.

McCarthy presents his dialogue like a play, dispensing with quotation marks. His contention being there's no reason to block a page up with marks if your writing is clear.

Try it if you wish. I'll stick to more traditional punctuation. And the evil twin of punctuation is dialogue structure - a serious stumbling block for many writers attempting to produce a page-turner.

It's technical stuff, so let's get it over with.

Lines of Dialogue/Paragraphs

New dialogue usually starts with a new paragraph. You can have dialogue - action - more dialogue or dialogue - *they said* - dialogue in the same paragraph. But the next interjection should be a new paragraph. And yet another paragraph for the next bit of dialogue.

It's not exactly a rule but it makes any story a hell of a lot easier to read.

"I gots some new dialogue to add," I said.

"I hope you aren't intending to include any of your ridiculous analogies, she replied.

I might." I scratched my head. "You see, analogies are like cars. They..."

I caught her warning glance.

"No. No analogies."

He/she Said Repeatedly is Boring

In his quest for simple clarity, Cormac McCarthy also gets rid of *he/she said*. (For brevity's sake I'll often refer to *they said* instead). I'm with him on that because I find lots of *they said* repetitive and a tad dull.

How do you get around it? The easiest method is to use alternatives.

Obviously, don't say things like *they expostulated*, or *they ululated*. However, there's nothing wrong with *they explained* or *they snapped*. Just use them in moderation.

He/she said **Placement**

You can also vary where you place *they said*. Move it from the end of the line to the middle of a long sentence, cutting it in two. It makes the reading smoother and breaks up larger dialogue chunks.

"Never in the field of human conflict has so much been owed by so many to so few," he said.

Becomes

"Never in the field of human conflict," he said. "Has so much been owed by so many to so few."

You can still put in an alternative too.

"Never in the field of human conflict," he thundered. "Has so much been owed by so many to so few."

Action Rather Than *he/she said*

You can also replace *they said* with physical gestures. Take this phrase, for instance:

"That possum took a bite out of my pants," he said. "I'll have to buy another pair." He turned and showed them his bum.

It flows better if you dump *they said* and break up the sentence with action instead.

"That possum took a bite out of my pants." He turned and showed them his bum. *"I'll have to buy another pair."*

Characters rarely stay perfectly still, so there are unlimited gestures they can make, even if it's something as simple as sitting down or wiping tears from their eyes.

Here's one mistake everybody makes. Putting in *they said* with an action attached.

"Never in the field of human conflict," he said, placing his glasses on the desk. *"Has so much been owed by so many to so few."*

You don't need both. Just the action.

"Never in the field of human conflict." He placed his glasses on the table. *"Has so much been owed by so many to so few."*

However you choose to alter the structure, cutting sentences into smaller chunks is always a good thing. Short back-and-forth works best. In real life, nobody manages huge soliloquies without being interrupted.

I know. I've tried.

Character Voice

If it sounds like writing I rewrite it.

Elmore Leonard

I won't rehash everything I've said about characters. I'll just remind you that if your character has a distinct voice, the reader will know who is talking because of the way they speak, getting rid of a lot of *they said* and its equivalents.

By voice, I mean any kind of distinction. Accent. Mannerisms. Attitude. While clumsy phraseology is not conducive to flowing and lively prose, it *can* be used to make dialogue more natural. If your character is a typical factory worker from Forfar, their grammar won't be perfect and they're not going to talk like an Oxford Don.

Here's an exchange from John Kennedy O Toole's *A Confederacy of Dunces* between the pompous hero, who is working as a hot dog vendor and an African American janitor.

"How come a white cat like you, talkin so good, sellin weenies?"

"Please blow your smoke elsewhere. My respiratory system, unfortunately, is below par. I suspect that

I am the result of particularly weak conception on the part of my father. His sperm was probably emitted in a rather offhand manner."

"You mus be outa your min man. You oughta have you a good job, big Buick, all that shit. Whoa! Air condition, colour TV..."

"I have a very pleasant occupation," Ignatius answered icily. "Outdoor work, no supervision. The only pressure is on the feet."

O Toole only uses one interjection - *Ignatius answered icily.* (not *Ignatius said*!). But we know exactly who is talking by the way they speak.

I've already suggested using one word to describe minor characters. Now have them talk in a way that reflects this. If they're an evasive sort, they won't answer a question directly. If they're self-obsessed, everything they say will revolve around them.

Let's put all this together.

Here's a bit of dialogue from *Burnt Out*. It has no *they said*, incorporates physical gestures slotted onto the middle of lines, short sentences and a new paragraph for each new piece of dialogue. It also has a character with a memorable name (though Courage Louviere is actually a real woman).

"We need to start working together as a team, Courage. Play to our strengths."

"Didn't say no, did I?"

"You're the only one who's properly mobile." Arthur *waved her away. "Go search the pool area and gymnasium. I need goggles and anything else floaty. Inflatable armbands would be best. And helmets. Elbow pads. Any protective equipment a sportsman might use."*

"Will do."

"Open the doors to the offices too."

"All right."

"And take the jackhammer. It's gas-powered, so it works without a compressor."

"Ok."

"You really don't talk much, do you?"

"Nope."

From this, you can tell Arthur is in charge and Courage is the strong, silent type. As the novel goes on and Courage begins to trust her companions, she becomes more voluble and, therefore, more vulnerable. In other words, you don't have to tell the reader that a character is changing. The dialogue can do it for you as well.

Show, don't tell.

Take Time Out Occasionally.

Dialogue should move the plot forwards. Unless you don't want it to.

Tension. Relax. Tension. Relax.

Take time out from the drama to relish wordplay. If your heroes are running for their lives, that's not really the time to discuss what's for dinner. If they manage to lock themselves in a room, use that to have them take stock of their situation and engage in a bit of tense banter. The danger hasn't gone away. You're just giving the readers a bit of breathing space and a chance to connect with the characters.

Or have some chit-chat for the sheer hell of it. After all, real people digress from the situation in hand all the time and conversations go off at all sorts of tangents.

Those non-sequitur moments may not advance the plot but they are a great way to bring your characters to life. The reader hangs out with them. Gets to know them.

Quentin Tarantino is excellent at this. The tipping argument from *Reservoir Dogs* or the burger discussion in *Pulp Fiction* are perfect examples. The repartee may not advance the plot one iota. It does tell us about the characters. More than that, it's a lot of fun.

I've already mentioned the *USS Indianapolis* conversation from *Jaws.* In a movie filled with toothy horror, this is the scariest scene, even though it doesn't feature the shark. Playful one-upmanship slowly morphs into a chilling monologue by shark hunter Quint.

It's a sideshow and ought to slow things down. Instead, it creates palpable tension and reveals the stoic Quint is actually driven by fear, hatred and guilt. It foreshadows a budding friendship that will be cut short because two of the men have no idea how much danger they are in - and the one who does can't quit. It ends with an invisible force hitting the boat and shattering the tension. An absolutely searing example of how good dialogue makes a story - and how slowing down the pace increases the effectiveness of the next big shock.

If you want to write a page-turner, you can't have *lots* of moments that aren't pertinent to the plot or don't advance the story. Don't ramble. However, if you think up a scene that is funny or poignant, even if it's not strictly relevant, keep it in.

Slot in flavouring at the appropriate moments. All good books and movies have a tense bit, then a reflective bit, then another tense bit. Remember My dodgy roller coaster analogy. Slowly up. Whiz down. Slowly up. Whiz down. Tension. Relax. Tension. Relax.

What you don't want to do is have characters wallow in exposition. They can tell each other facts but not share information they both already know, simply to inform the reader.

Nor should you put in a non-pertinent scene, explanation or snatch of dialogue when the book is moving swiftly. That will slow things down in a bad way, like that roller coaster screeching down the slope and hitting a giant wad of chewing gum.

God, the analogy is getting worse.

Humour

We've established that, as well as moving the plot along, dialogue can allow readers to spend quality time with your characters. The best dialogue makes you *want* to spend quality time with them. And, as in real life, we want to hang out with people who are fun.

Humans say amusing things, often at inappropriate moments. Unless you've deliberately made your hero an actuary or call centre worker, they're going to say some humorous stuff. This will make them more likeable and I guarantee readers will appreciate that levity, even in a serious novel. I can't stress this enough.

Don't be po-faced with your dialogue. Seriously.

As I said, movies are especially good for studying dialogue. I'd suggest watching a couple of classic comedies and ignoring everything but the flow of speech. You don't need to turn your characters into The Stooges. Just throw the reader a funny line now and then.

Even better, watch dramas with sparking dialogue. Aaron Sorkin is a master. So is Lawrence Kasdan. Ditto the films of Howard Hawks, Wes Anderson and Cameron Crowe.

This is even more true of plays which completely stand or fall on their dialogue. So here's my next tip.

Treat your dialogue like a play.

Read it out loud. See if it rolls off the tongue. If you have accommodating friends, get them in on the act. Literally. Get them to pretend to be the characters and act out the dialogue.

You'll be amazed at how different what you've written sounds when spoken aloud. You'll soon see what you need to change to be more entertaining and authentic.

Exercise 6

Take a chapter from your novel or an entire short story.

Write it as a play.

The Ending

You're coming to the end of your journey. Hopefully you've penned something pretty damned readable and now you're in the home stretch. This is often when self-doubt rears its ugly head, though it's a bit late now.

While you want the whole story to be fantastic, two parts have to stand out, the beginning and the end. We've already addressed the former but let's quickly revisit it.

Your beginning was probably written some time ago, so now you can look at it with the benefit of hindsight. The story is laid out in front of you, almost fully formed. Does the start still hold true? Is it setting the reader up properly for what comes next? If you've been altering stuff as you go along (and you should) all that's required are few tweaks.

If not, make the changes and check to see if there's a knock-on effect. Are there more questions and answers you can put in? Ones that didn't occur to you at the time because you didn't exactly know where the story was headed. This is your last chance to fix things.

Once you've finished tearing out your hair and sorting the timeline, tackle the conclusion. You've started with a bang and you have to finish with one.

If you've taken my advice, you've had a rough ending all along. It may have changed several times as the story progressed but that's par for the course. I cannot recall a single instance when I used my own original finale. As my novels unfold, I'll ponder another ending, then another. Usually, I have almost reached the end before the right one presents itself.

Don't shoehorn in the finish you planned if it no longer fits what has come before, no matter how much you love it. You've taken the reader on a journey. Accept that, after all the twists and turns, you may not end up where you once expected to go.

And in Book 62…

You may be writing a novel series. If so, don't finish with a cliffhanger. It's not fair to your readers. They've taken the plunge with you and deserve a proper resolution. Wrap everything up and answer all the questions raised in this particular book. If the audience enjoyed your story, they'll want to read the next one - but don't force them to by not providing a satisfactory climax. Also, should you be lucky enough to get a publisher, you never can tell when they'll pull the plug.

My book *Secret City* was the first part of the *Galhadria* trilogy. The second, *Hunting Charlie Wilson,* ended on a cliffhanger. The publisher declined to commission the third and I'm still pissed off I ended it that way. Eventually, I had to write and self-publish the last part myself just to get closure.

If your book is part of a series, the best thing you can do is answer all the questions and then raise one completely new one at the end. *Secret City* had a final battle where the hero kills the villain, Mordred. In the epilogue, Mordred's mother appears. It's not cheating, as the mother hasn't been mentioned up until this point. But now the reader knows what the sequel will be about. Her revenge.

In a series, epilogues are damned useful. The story is finished but the epilogue tells you what to expect from the sequel.

On one level, ending your story is straightforward. Answer all the questions you raised. Solve the mystery. Unite the lovers. However, resolving the plot isn't enough. You need emotional impact too. Perhaps even philosophical portent.

Tension. Relax. Tension. Relax. The ending is where the roller coaster finally stops. The point when you put the brakes on for good and pause to reflect. It's your sign-off. The story's eulogy. You want to leave the reader with a lump in their throat. Have them punch the air and shout "Yeah!" Leave them thinking about the implications of what has transpired long after they close the last page.

In short, the ending should be unforgettable. We'll look more closely at that soon. First, at the risk of being too obvious, here are the main climactic choices.

Happy Endings

A happy ending gives readers exactly what they want and often what they expect. I say give them a little more than they expect.

A happy ending can be poignant too. Here's the last line from *The House at Pooh Corner* by A. A. Milne.

But wherever they go, and whatever happens to them on the way, in that enchanted place on the top of the Forest a little boy and his Bear will always be playing.

Splendid. Happy but still brings a tear to the eye.

Sad Endings

Ending on a negative emotion may piss some people off, but there's no denying the powerful impact of sad endings. Read George Orwell's *1984* for evidence. Great for stories that have a 'message', though.

As with happy endings, I think you can give a little more than a basic downer. A bittersweet ending works best for me. This usually involves the hero losing but remaining an inspiration. Or winning at huge personal cost.

The Open Ending

I like open endings myself. You get out of trouble by letting the *readers* decide if it is happy or sad. What does Bob say to Charlotte at the finale of *Lost in Translation?* It's up to the viewer. Or, take Margaret Mitchell's last line in *Gone With The Wind.*

I'll go home. And I'll think of some way to get him back. After all... tomorrow is another day.

Will Scarlet get Rhett back? Maybe. Maybe not. Quantum Mechanics 101. You fill in the blanks.

The Shocking/Subversive/Twist Ending

Subverting expectations will also provoke a huge response, though you have to be careful it's not one of horror. Be bold (that should be my catchphrase).

At the end of *The Kirkfallen Stopwatch,* the three heroes intend to try and prevent war by killing all the other children on their island. And that finale was toned down from the original, where they give up and commit suicide. *Atonement* by Ian McEwan turns a triumphant love story into utter tragedy with an ending you don't see coming.

Not that subversive twists need to be unhappy. In the *Armageddon Twins,* the hero finds out all her memories are fake and she is an AI in a cloned body. Instead of being devastated, she thinks it makes her cool.

Whatever ending you choose, there are a couple of devices you must avoid.

The Deus Ex Machina

This is something else I can't pronounce. It's a Latin term from ancient Greek and Roman theatre - *God from the machine*.- where an actor dressed like a deity would be lowered from a crane to solve characters' problems.

A deus ex machina, then, is an unlikely story event that provides a quick, all-too-convenient resolution and usually feels contrived. Shakespeare uses this device in *As You Like It*. So does J. K. Rowling in *Harry Potter and the Chamber of Secrets* - where a doomed Harry is conveniently saved by the sudden appearance of a magical Phoenix.

C'mon. You can do better than Shakespeare and J. K. Rowling.

The Info Dump

Resist having a huge amount of explanation at the end - the dreaded info dump. Agatha Christie may get away with it but the rest of us won't.

Let's go back to our dreadful constructing a wardrobe analogy. You've finished it, yet discover you still have a few screws and one plank left over. You can't just throw them into the wardrobe, close the door and hope nobody will notice.

It's the same with your story. If you end up with a heap of information, revelations or explanations that haven't been fully dealt with, don't bung them all down at the climax. Keep the best bit, then go back and find ways to thread the rest naturally into the story. It's painstaking but worth it.

Parting is Such Sweet Sorrow

I believe readers get more out of the ending if you emphasise the character arc over the narrative one.

Naturally, I want the audience to close my book and say *that was a great plot!* However, it's the emotional response I go after when I reach the finale. The reader is saying goodbye to characters they care about and you should play mercilessly on that. Apply every skill in your arsenal.

You can use context.

The Princess Bride ends with a plain old *As you wish.* Pretty dull, huh? Until you remember the ways this phrase is used earlier in the story. Then it has real poignancy.

You can use homage.

In *A Town Called Library,* the heroes sit astride their horses on a hilltop, overlooking the village they have saved from overwhelming odds. One decides to stay and become a farmer. The others turn and ride into the sunset.

Yup. It's a shameless reworking of the *Magnificent Seven* which is, in turn, a remake of Kurosawa's *Seven Samurai*. By association, my finale now had the added emotion heft of two epic endings to two beloved movies.

You can use symbolism and imagery.

Look at how they are applied in F. Scott Fitzgerald's *The Great Gatsby*.

Gatsby believed in the green light, the orgiastic future that year by year recedes before us. It eluded us then, but that's no matter—tomorrow we will run faster, stretch out our arms farther. And one fine morning...

So we beat on, boats against the current, borne back ceaselessly into the past.

One of the great endings of all time. The image of boats beating against the current is perfect and 'the Green light' is now universally symbolic of the things we wish to achieve.

It is almost overshadowed by my favourite short story, *Flowers for Algernon,* by Daniel Keyes (Algernon is a lab mouse). Written in the form of a diary, the killer idea and narrative arc couldn't be plainer. Charlie is a man with severe learning difficulties. An experimental drug turns him into a genius. Then he slowly regresses.

The character arc is something else entirely. Charlie's newfound intelligence means he finally understands how badly he has been treated by 'friends' in the past. Now he is too smart (though still not socially adept enough) to establish relationships or enjoy his new life. When he finally returns to the way he was, he writes this last diary entry.

Its a good feeling to know things and be smart. I wish I had it rite now if I did I would sit down and reed all the time. Anyway I bet Im the first dumb person in the world who ever found out somthing importent for sience. I remember I did somthing but I dont remember what. So I gess its like I did it for all the dumb pepul like me. Good-by Miss Kinnian and Dr Strauss and evreybody. And P.S. please tell Dr Nemur not to be such a grouch when pepul laff at him and he woud have more frends. Its easy to make frends if you let pepul laff at you. Im going to have lots of frends where I go. P.P.S. Please if you get a chanse put some flowrs on Algernons grave in the bak yard.

See what Keys does here? He gives Charlie a happy ending. Because he *is* happy again. For the rest of us, it is a devastatingly sad ending. The reader understands all the wonderful things Charlie will never appreciate. They know he will once more be pitied and dehumanised - the butt of his 'friend's' jokes.

It's both thought-provoking and emotionally crushing. Genius.

The Last Line

You started with a killer idea, so end with a killer last line. I can't tell you what it might be but I recommend you deliberately write any old thing to begin with. It'll bug you so much you won't stop thinking about it until, two weeks later, a flawless one will occur to you. Use the same ticks. Symbolism. Homage. Context.

In *Spiral Wood,* the hero's last words are, "Life is beautiful, isn't it?"

Which seems like a very positive thing to say until you factor in context. You realise he is genuinely asking the question, not making a rhetorical statement - a subversion that encapsulates both his misplaced hopefulness and inner emptiness.

I was rather proud of that. Then I realised I had a plot flaw, so I had to add on another three chapters.

Not everyone gets a happy ever after.

Exercise 7

Take the ending for any short story or book you are working on. If it has a happy ending, make it sad. If it has a sad ending, make it open. If it has an open ending, make it happy.

You get the picture.

Revision

Can we fix it? Yes, we can!

Bob the Builder

As I stated earlier, I'm a big advocate of getting as much right as possible in the first draft. If you pull that off, revision is merely a tidying-up process rather than a creative one. As a developmental editor, however, I'll often take a writer's draft and make some fairly drastic suggestions. I may recommend changing the structure, losing a character, altering the ending or adding and subtracting subplots.

I'm not around, so you'll have to tackle that nightmare yourself. It requires a level of objectivity that's not present when you're immersed in writing. When you revise, try to separate yourself from any attachment to your plot, prose, dialogue and characters.

Use quantum mechanics. Everything is fluid until your last forensic, impartial observation.

Major Alterations

If you do decide to embark on major alterations, you have my sympathy. At this late stage, the process requires a lot of teeth gnashing. You may not even be sure the changes will improve your story. Until you see the results, it's hard to judge whether you've made things better or not.

Here's what you do.

Save your draft. Then make the major changes and save it again under another file name. Compare both and see which version you like best. That's your new draft. Repeat until you are satisfied you can't improve it any more.

It's time-consuming and frustrating but there's no easy way around it. That's another reason to make your first draft as perfect as you can, working out any big changes as you go along.

Streamlining

When you finally have the story optimally structured, it's time to move on to the streamlining/cosmetic process.

Obviously, you want to write as well as you can from the get-go. But the alterations I'm going to suggest can easily be done with a finished manuscript. In many ways, it's actually better if you make these changes post story, rather than breaking concentration and slowing the flow when you're actually writing.

Besides, this is the bit I find most fun. You've built your wardrobe. Now you get to pimp it up. Varnish the wood and add some fancy handles.

Of course, nothing is that easy. You really ought to go over the advice in the prose section again and apply that too. Whether you do or not, here's the final run-through you should make.

Take out Ultra-Long Sentences.

A mixture of short and medium sentences works best, with only the occasional long burst. I've said it before and I'll say it again, short is always better than long.

If you are in the habit of breaking up a long sentence with commas, use full stops instead. Ditto colons and semi colons. Replace them with full stops.

What of dashes, I hear you cry? Strictly speaking, double dashes are used to interrupt a complete sentence. The sentence will still work without the phrase inside the dashes. It's important - or it wouldn't be there - but not essential to the flow of your story. Commas, on the other hand, enclose phrases that belong in the flow of your sentence.

I tend to play exceedingly fast and loose with these rules, putting dashes and commas where I think they look appropriate. Just don't mix the two together. The sequence should be dash-phrase-dash and comma-phrase-comma. You *can* put both sequences in one sentence but that would make it pretty long - something we are trying to avoid.

The moral. When in doubt, just use a full stop and start a new sentence.

The way to break up long sentences in dialogue is to insert *they said* or an equivalent word or action. However, if I was to say that again, I'd be repeating myself. And you should never repeat yourself.

Got that? Never repeat yourself.

Repetition

The ear tends to be lazy, craves the familiar and is shocked by the unexpected; the eye, on the other hand, tends to be impatient, craves the novel and is bored by repetition.

W. H. Auden

Repetition is so common it's endemic. *Do not* keep repeating the same words and phrases. It's ungainly and looks unprofessional.

The dog stared at him. He knew he couldn't escape the dog by running. The dog would easily catch him. The dog snarled again.

"Good dog," he said. "Please don't kill me.
The dog moved forward.

Who let those dogs out? That's too many dogs! (I can use an exclamation mark here cause I'm shouting inside).

Just use a different word. Alternate dog with *it* or *hound* or *pooch* or *animal* or *creature* or *Doberman*. It's as simple as that. Cut out repetition by substituting other words instead.

The best way to spot recurrence is to use 'find' or 'replace' in Microsoft Word - to see how often, in quick succession, the same word comes up. Even if you write in longhand you'll eventually type your manuscript, so there's no excuse.

Repetition does not only apply to single words but phrases as well. From short ones like *of course* and *you know* to actions like *she shrugged her shoulders* or *he ran a hand through his hair*.

It often crops up at the beginning of sentences, with words that don't really need to be there. For instance, *well* or *so*. I'm guilty of this particular affectation myself, even in this book where I actively tried to cut them all out.

These are common iterations but each writer has their own particular additional foibles. Ask friends to point them out specifically and deal with them.

Expletives (see **Expletives**), also known as 'crutch words', are frequently repeated. If you recall, these are words that do not change the meaning of the sentence and don't have any real reason to be there. The good news is, it means they can be deleted rather than replaced with an alternative.

Here are some of the usual suspects to give you a feel for them.

Seemed to. Almost. Just. Felt like. A bit. Really. Actually. Definitely. As though. Slightly. Somehow. Realized.

My least favourites are *that* and *had*. Use word check and you'll be amazed how often you've used them. I reckon they can go 70% of the time.

All right, I made that figure up. But it's a lot.

And there is literally never a case for using *literally*.

Repetition is a pet peeve of mine, so I may be a bit dictatorial about it. I was hoist on my own petard when writing *Burnt Out* and discovered there aren't that many alternatives for the word 'fire'. Blaze, conflagration, flames and inferno. That's about it. I had to jump through hoops - flaming ones - to not repeat myself.

This forced me to get creative. I used harbingers like *smoke* and *glow* to show when the fire was coming or had the characters do their best to avoid encountering the blaze. Tried to see through their eyes, which were often filled with smoke. Concentrated on the material being destroyed rather than the flames.

Turns out this improved the book, as I realised I wasn't writing about fire itself but about what it *does*.

Cutting

The number 1. The biggie.

An editor will usually cut your manuscript, no matter how good it is, often to your disappointment. There are two ways to approach this.

One. Let them. They need to feel useful. Two. Sort it yourself.

It's your story and you should be the one to pare it down. A good writer is never afraid to savagely cut their own work.

Less is more.

In case I haven't stressed this enough, here's cutting advice from some of the greats.

The most valuable of all talents is that of never using two words when one will do.

Thomas Jefferson

Whenever you feel an impulse to perpetrate a piece of exceptionally fine writing, obey it - wholeheartedly - and delete it before sending your manuscript to press. Murder your darlings.

Arthur Quiller-Couch

If it sounds like writing, I rewrite it. Or, if proper usage gets in the way, it may have to go. I can't allow what we learned in English composition to disrupt the sound and rhythm of the narrative.

Elmore Leonard

Kill your darlings, kill your darlings, even when it breaks your egocentric little scribbler's heart, kill your darlings... When you write a story, you are telling yourself the story. When you rewrite, your main job is taking out all the things that are NOT the story...

Stephen King

Sit down and put down everything that comes into your head and then you're a writer. But an author is one who can judge his own stuff's worth, without pity, and destroy most of it.

Sidonie Gabrielle Colette

Writing is not like painting where you add... Writing is more like a sculpture where you remove, you eliminate in order to make the work visible. Even those pages you remove somehow remain. There is a difference between a book of two hundred pages which is the result of an original eight hundred pages. The six hundred pages are there. Only you don't see them.

Elie Wiesel

Read over your compositions and whenever you meet with a passage which you think is particularly fine, strike it out.

Samuel Johnson

Let the reader find that he cannot afford to omit any line of your writing because you have omitted every word that he can spare.

Ralph Waldo Emerson

Learn to enjoy this tidying process. I don't like to write; I like to have written. But I love to rewrite. I especially like to cut: to press the DELETE key and see an unnecessary word or phrase or sentence vanish into the electricity.

William Zinsser

I believe more in the scissors than I do in the pencil.

Truman Capote

Not a wasted word. This has been the main point to my literary thinking all my life.

Hunter S. Thompson

So the writer who breeds more words than he needs, is making a chore for the reader who reads.

Dr. Seuss

What exactly do you cut? Everything. Repetition. Crutch words. Adverbs. Adjectives. Cliches. Bits of prose you cut and pasted from elsewhere. Long sentences. Exposition. Stuff you added cause it sounded great, not because it fit. Description. More description.

Pare your story down. It's what the world's best writers do. Even better, it's what the world's most readable writers do.

Exercise 8

Take any short story or chapter from a novel you are working on or have written.

Cut it down by 50%.

Proofreading

Hopefully, you formatted your novel as you went along. If you haven't, it's no biggie. Do it now (see **Formatting**). That just leaves the final stage in the process. Proofreading. Correcting spelling, punctuation and other related minutiae.

Many writers hire a proofreader at this point but that can be expensive. If you are lucky enough to find a publisher, their own editor should spot small mistakes. If you are self-publishing or simply want your copy to be its very best, here are a few tips on that.

One. Use the Microsoft Word spell checker. That's a no-brainer. If you have Grammarly, great, and the free version is fine. I think ProWritingAid is even better, though I only use the grammar section for either. I don't always agree with their suggestions and neither should you. They are guides, not rules. Don't let an algorithm dictate how you write.

Two. Use Microsoft Word Reader to read the story aloud. As you listen, you'll hear mistakes you didn't spot on the page. It's best to have your phone read it out with another copy of the manuscript open on a laptop. That way, you can correct as you go along. You'll also spot clumsy sentences and repetition this way.

Three. Print out the manuscript and read it backwards. Because you do not see it as a story, you'll spot punctuation mistakes more easily.

Four. Give it to a friend who is pedantic.

Exercise 9

I have left a very small number of punctuation, spelling and grammatical mistakes in this manual.
See if you can find them.

Nobody Knows Anything

There are no rules. There are paradigms, conventions, patterns. Know them but don't let them constrain your creativity.

Bong Joon Ho

In this section, I'll be referring to books and book publishers. However, the same advice broadly applies to short stories and online or physical magazines and anthologies.

The screenwriter William Goldman said:

Nobody knows anything...... Not one person in the entire motion picture field knows for a certainty what's going to work. Every time out it's a guess and, if you're lucky, an educated one.

He's talking about movies but the same is true of books. And of Goldman himself, who wrote screenplays for *All the President's Men*, *Butch Cassidy and the Sundance Kid* and *The Princess Bride,* then utter guff like *Wild Card* and *Dreamcatcher*.

Everything is subjective. When I finished *Bunker 10,* I sent it to the Scottish Arts Council to see if I could get a grant. They told me, in no uncertain terms, it was a dreadful book. Badly written and totally unsuitable for young adults. Their suggestion? That I scrap it and write something else.

Jesus. A simple *no* would have sufficed.

I ignored them, sent it to an agent without changing a word and she sold it to Oxford University Press. It went on to be short-listed for The Angus Book Award, the South Lanarkshire Book Award, The RED Award, the Stockport Book Prize and won the Royal Mail Award - Britain's biggest children's book prize.

I trust I don't have to elaborate on the moral of that story.

The point I'm making is that the opinions of others, even so-called experts, aren't necessarily correct. Especially when it comes to writing 'rules'.

The Rules of Writing.

I have seen the following ten popular bits of advice in various writing guides and websites. They are decent enough but not stuff I ever really consider when I write a novel. Following them slavishly is also rather confining, so I don't think they are all that useful.

One. Give your book 3 acts. Some writers (especially romance ones) restrict this even further.

Act 1=25%, Act II=50%, Act III=25%

Two. Think of the main point your story will make. Everything else should be in service to this point.

Three. Begin with your main character's goal. This should be something big and you must give a good reason why they want it.

Four. Make sure your theme carries all the way through the novel. I've already poo-pooed this one in a previous section.

Five. Make sure each of your scenes has a clear goal.

Six. Do plenty of foreshadowing. I've covered this too. Sure, you can - but at your own discretion.

Seven. Don't make your characters passive or reactive. Make them proactive. Yes, it's more exciting that way. It's also less realistic. How about making them proactive *most* of the time? Say 70%.

All right, I made that figure up too.

Eight. Don't use low or muddled stakes.

Nine. Begin your book in the middle of the action or 'in medias res' (Latin for *in the midst of things*).

Ten. Your story's 'inciting incident' (an event that sends your protagonist's story in a different direction) should occur no more than 10% into the book.

Like I say, none of these are bad bits of advice, except for number 10 - which I think is daft. But there are plenty of good stories that don't follow them.

In writing there are no rules, only suggestions.

Even my favourite pet peeve: *don't repeat yourself,* can be ignored in certain circumstances. If you're writing about a character descending into paranoia, replicating the same words may be an effective way of portraying that. What I'm getting at is this. If you genuinely think your novel will benefit from an approach that flies in the face of all perceived wisdom, don't be put off. It may not work but I've nothing but admiration for someone who tries something daring.

Besides, times change and so do trends. While you shouldn't let rules or the market dictate the way you write, there's no harm in getting ahead of the curve. The manly, protective male and swooning female are still staples of the romance genre. Yet I'm betting (and hoping) this will soon become an anachronism readers see as the relic of a bygone age.

Don't be afraid to rebel. Just make sure you recognise that what you are doing *is* rebellion and not simply bad writing.

Traditional Publishing

Talking of markets and bad writing, publishers, agents and editors can be completely wrong too. I'd go as far as to say they're often wrong. *Harry Potter and the Philosopher's Stone* by J K Rowling was dismissed dozens of times before being accepted. The first *Sherlock Holmes* story was rejected by Blackwoods because 18-year-old Arthur Conan Doyle didn't enclose a stamped addressed envelope. Own goal!

There's a time to follow advice but also a time to stick to your guns. It depends on how strongly you feel. I mentioned *A Confederacy of Dunces* earlier and it's a sad example. It was the only novel by John Kennedy O Toole, who couldn't sell it and eventually committed suicide - which is a bit extreme, even for a writer.

His mum then tried to get it published for nine years, to no avail. She finally arrived at the office of the author and editor Percy Walker, handed him the manuscript and insisted he read it. Walker reluctantly gave in, knowing he'd be able to tell its worth from the first few pages. Here's what he said:

In this case I read on. And on. First with the sinking feeling that it was not bad enough to quit, then with a prickle of interest, then a growing excitement, and finally an incredulity: surely it was not possible that it was so good.

He got it published in 1980 and immediately won the Pulitzer Prize. If nothing else, this demonstrates the importance of having a beginning that makes the reader want to keep going. And of not committing suicide.

Even if you do get a contract, your battle isn't over. My friend Keith Grey is a multi-award winner but had to fight with his publisher for years to keep the original ending for one of his books.

In *Father Figure,* the romance between the two main characters ends with twenty pages still to go and the emphasis changes to a minor character. No publisher was going to accept that, so I brought it out myself. I'm not saying it's the best ending the book could have. It's certainly not the most commercial. But it was the ending *I* wanted.

When it comes to traditional publishing, however, you'll often have to compromise. Either before your story gets accepted or in order for it to be released. Nor do you want a reputation for being 'difficult'.

You must decide how malleable you're going to be but here's a neat trick. An editor will often suggest alternatives to what you've written. You can say: *No, that's a really stupid idea* and I have often been tempted to do so. Or you can accept they may have a point and say: *Yes, I'll most certainly change it.*

That does not mean you should make the changes they suggest. Instead, come up with your own alternative. Editors are good at spotting what doesn't work but not always great at fixing it. They may well be open to using your new option rather than theirs.

You might not feel this is something you can get away with. If so, write two versions, just in case you end up self-publishing. Don't be bullied into producing something you hate.

In the end, it's your damned story, isn't it?

I've been rather critical of editors. In all honesty, though, the best ones are invaluable. The novels of F. Scott Fitzgerald were almost a collaboration with his editor, Maxwell Perkins, who red-penned his work mercilessly. He did the same with Ernest Hemmingway and cut Thomas Wolfe's novel *Look Homeward, Angel* by 90,000 words. That's right. 90,000. And he was right in each case.

T.S. Elliot's *The Wasteland* is considered one of the pinnacles of English Literature. But it was edited by the poet Ezra Pound who wrote things in the margin like this:

Too tum-pum at a stretch; too penty (too much iambic pentameter)*; too loose; Perhaps be damned; make up yr. mind; verse not interesting enough to warrant so much of it* and *Too easy.*

Synopsis and Covering Letter

We'll get to self-publishing soon. Right now, let's assume you are going for a traditional publisher or an agent. You may wonder what the difference is.

An agent is just a middleman. You can pitch your book directly to a publisher but they are more likely to look at a submission made on your behalf by an agent - especially larger publishing houses. So, go for an agent first. Though they take a commission, that's OK.

If your book doesn't make any money, you haven't lost much. If it does, you won't care.

If you can't bag an agent, smaller presses are more amenable to being approached directly. *The Writers and Artists Yearbook* is a great source for this. To keep things brief, I will refer to publishers and agents as 'publishers' for the rest of this section.

You might have written a masterpiece. If you don't send a decent covering letter/synopsis (and follow the publisher's submission guidelines), it may never get looked at.

A cover letter introduces you and then tells the publisher about the book. The genre. Why it will sell. Who the audience is. What kind of popular novels are similar. Keep it to a page. If the book is part of a series, you'll have to elaborate a little on what happens in later books and how many there are. You will also have to tell them *specifically* who the audience is and their age range.

You'll also need a synopsis. If you can capture everything in 300 words, that's usually a good length. Irritating as it may be, you have to give away the ending. I hate doing it as well - but it's protocol.

While a synopsis and covering letter are essential, I recommend doing a few variations on these.

The High Concept Pitch

High concept. Having a striking and easily communicable idea.

If you're lucky, your killer idea can be described in a couple of sentences that will make others go, "Hell yeah!" High concepts are usually associated with film and it was the director Steven Spielberg who said:

If a person can tell me the idea in 25 words or less, it's going to make a pretty good movie.

However, high concept will work just as well for books. Commercially speaking, the best killer ideas are those short ones publishers can't resist. As I stated, they don't have to be original but a cool twist on something that already exists.

This example really demonstrates the effectiveness of the high concept killer idea. It also shows how money is an overriding factor in the entertainment industry of which publishing, like it or not, is a part. Any agent will accept a badly written book if they think it will still sell. *Fifty Shades of Grey*, I'm looking at you.

The film *Jaws* was a massive hit in the 1970s. On the back of that, the movie *Alien* was sold with one tiny phrase - *Jaws in Space*. An awesome high concept idea. The outline for its sequel was even simpler - in fact, it's regarded as the shortest successful pitch in film history.

James Cameron had written a treatment for *Alien 2* that nobody would touch because the original, though lauded, wasn't a massive financial success. Cameron walked into the studio boardroom without so much as a piece of paper. He went to a chalkboard and wrote the word ALIEN. Then he added an 'S' to make AL-IENS. Dramatically, he drew two vertical lines through the S, turning it into ALIEN$. He turned around and grinned.

The project was green-lit that day for $18 million.

That's a fantasy for most of us. However, if you can describe your book in one dynamic sentence, you can use it along with your synopsis as a sales pitch.

Taglines

A tagline is a short, catchy slogan that piques interest and looks great on the cover of your book. It can take a long time to get this perfect but it's a worthwhile mental exercise. Coincidentally, *Alien* had a classic.

In space no one can hear you scream.

The tagline for *A Town Called Library* took me almost as long to think up as the book itself.

Once upon a time… it was the end.

Loglines.

A logline is a one-sentence summary or description that distils the important elements of your screenplay. (Protagonist. Central Conflict. Antagonist. Setup) into a clear, concise teaser. Though they are more used in the film industry than publishing, you may as well think a logline up, just in case an agent or publisher asks. My logline for *The Armageddon Twins* is a bit clunky but sure packs in the info!

A grumpy teenage loner who can copy any skill and a chirpy motormouth who can't remember her past must stop Armageddon - helped by a selfish con man, a homicidal convict and a rogue artificial intelligence - each with their own hidden agenda.

Blurb

The blurb is best described as the paragraphs that go on the back of your book jacket or in the info section of your online eBook. Longer than a logline but shorter than a full synopsis, it captures the essence of what the book is about and why you are going to enjoy it. Here's mine from *Bunker 10*.

Beneath Pinewood research facility is Bunker 10, holding the two most dangerous creatures on earth. A little girl and a mouse.

Now they've escaped.

I recommend you do the exercises below, even if you missed out the other assignments. It helps to get the story straight in your head and you may actually use all of them!

Exercise 10

Pitch your story in one sentence (High Concept).
Write a logline.
Write a blurb. This is what would appear on the back cover if you saw it in a bookstore.
Write a page-long synopsis.

Self-Publishing

Traditional publishing is one avenue to get your stories out there. The other is to self-publish. You can do this if agents and commissioning editors don't recognise your genius or because you want to have creative and commercial control of your work.

At one time, self-publishing was costly and difficult and the finished product could be subpar. The likes of Amazon and Ingram Spark changed all that. There was also a stigma attached. Self-published writers were considered inferior to those who used a traditional publisher.

Again, that has changed. Yes, there are a lot of bad self-published books out there but I know authors who have turned down respectable traditional contracts to do their own thing. In many cases, you can make more money that way and nobody tells you to turn your main character from a six-foot detective into a four-foot nun.

I was a traditionalist for a long time but didn't like the drawbacks. Agents wanted me to write to a template. If I stuck to my guns, I found it hard to attract publishers. When I did, they had no idea how to market me. I got plenty of rave reviews but few sales, so I started to self-publish.

I'll give you a warning right now. If that's your chosen path, you have to mercilessly publicize yourself or you won't get rich. However, as I said at the beginning of this manual, I'm not in the writing business for money or fame. I write because I love it and my main goal is to continually improve and help others do the same. That's the reason I became an editor.

There are plenty of methods and outlets to help you self-publish. I'm not comparethemarket.com so I'll just make a few comments on how I do it as an example. By the way, I taught myself in a week and I'm a technological idiot, so you really can manage everything yourself.

I convert my Microsoft Word document to convert the manuscript to an eBook on Amazon Kindle and publish it on Kindle Direct.

I format the book for hard cover using the company Book Design Templates. I draw a rough approximation of what I want on the cover and have a Greek designer (Book Design Stars) jazz it up and size it. Nowadays, AI can also create fantastic covers but that's a can of worms I'm not going to open here. I upload both the cover and a PDF of the manuscript to Ingram Spark, then order however many hard copies I need. There are variations on this process but it's cheap, easy and works for me.

There's no need to use a vanity press and NEVER go with a publisher who asks you to pay anything.

There's a lot more to self-publishing but that's the basics. Now you just have to market your story, approach bookstores to stock it, post endlessly on social media and use sites like Book Bub and Book Funnel. How to do *that* successfully is advice for a different kind of expert.

Instead, I'll leave you with a cautionary tale.

There was once a songwriting trio called Stock, Aiken and Waterman, who wrote for the likes of Jason Donovan, Kylie Minogue, Dead or Alive and Rick Astley. All their songs sounded exactly the same but they were big hits because SA&W had hit on a winning formula and a great marketing strategy. Then some of the acts decided they had been pigeonholed and left to write their own ditties. It was the last time they bothered the song charts.

That's the problem with striking out on your own. *Nobody knows anything* applies to you too. You may be utterly wrong about how well your literary baby works, hard as it is to hear.

You *can* hire a professional editor like me and that's something many writers recommend. Even though I'm an editor, I still send work to friends and ask their opinion. Their opinion is that, being Scottish, I probably became an editor to save on the cost of hiring one.

I also recommend joining writing groups, even if it's only on Facebook. Give your story to people to beta read. If you get mixed messages, you have to decide which advice to take. But if every single reader says a scene is confusing or the story is too slow, they're probably right. Ignoring everyone transforms from confidence in your own ability to being pig-headed. Know when to back down and rethink.

I happen to think I'm superb at analogies. I really do. However, I have been mocked so often I am forced to accept they may not be my strong suit. Either that or the world is simply not ready for my genius.

I'll come clean. Anyone can pen a story. If you've put down 50,000 words, you've written a novel. Not everyone can write a good novel, however, or produce a page-turner. It's the same as drawing or painting. Learning the techniques won't turn you into Leonardo Da Vinci. I've done my best to give you a useful manual - a template, examples and writing tips. But here's the most important piece of advice I can impart.

DO NOT GIVE UP.

If you write a story and everyone agrees it's absolute garbage, write another. Then another.

I mentored a girl who kept sending me her work. It was dreadful. Really awful. She wasn't a good writer. Yet she was so determined I didn't have the heart to put her off, so I kept offering advice. Then, one day, she sent me a new story. With the usual feeling of doomed resignation, I read it.

This one was brilliant. Absolutely brilliant.

What did she do that was different? I've no idea. I don't think she did either. But she suddenly 'got it' whatever that indefinable thing is. I'd written her off as having no talent and now I looked like a doofus.

Writing something that sucks doesn't mean you lack the capacity to be great. Being rejected by publishers doesn't necessarily mean your writing sucks. It means the publisher doesn't think it's commercial.

Commercial success is wonderful, of course, But it can't be your driving force. You may hunger for fame and fortune, follow fads and trends or try to jump on the latest literary bandwagon. Don't do it at the expense of your own creativity and enjoyment.

If you love writing, stick with it and do it your way. Who's to say that won't make you a household name?

After all, nobody knows anything.

References

Banks, Iain. *The Wasp Factory.* Simon & Schuster 1998.

Brontë, Charlotte. *Jane Eyre.* Penguin 2003.

Carter, MJ. *The Strangler Vine.* Penguin Books 2014.

Christie, Agatha. *Murder on the Orient Express.* HarperCollins 2007.

Dickens, Charles. *Oliver Twist.* Penguin Books 2003. *A Christmas Carol.* Bethany House Publishers 1999.

Fitzgerald, F. Scott. *The Great Gatsby.* Penguin Press 2008.

Hart, Jack. *Storycraft: The Complete Guide to Writing Narrative Nonfiction.* University of Chicago Press 2012.

Henderson, Jan-Andrew. *The Armageddon Twins.* Floris Books 2018. Black Hart 2022. *Galhadria: The Charlie Wilson Trilogy.* Black Hart 2022. *I Don't Really Get Jan-Andrew Henderson.* Black Hart 2020. *Father Figure.* Black Hart 2020. *A Town Called Library.* Black Hart 2020. *Carnage.* Amberley Publishing 2020. *Burnt Out.* Black Hart 2020. *Hide.* Black Hart 2019. *Goners.* Black Hart 2019. *The Kirkfallen Stopwatch.* Oxford University Press 2009. Oetinger Publishers, Germany 2009. Black Hart 2019. *Waiting For A Train That Never Comes.* Oxford University Press 2008. Black Hart 2019. *Bunker 10* Oxford University Press 2007

Harcourt Inc, USA. Mlada Fronta, Czech Republic 2007. Black Hart 2019.

Keyes, Daniel. *Flowers for Algernon.* Gateway 2000.

King, Steven. *On Writing.* Hodder Paperbacks 2012.

Koontz, Dean. R. *How to Write Best Selling Fiction.* Writer's Digest Books 1981.

Lamott, Anne. *Bird by Bird: Some Instructions on Writing and Life.* Knopf 2014.

Lehane, Dennis. *Gone Baby Gone.* William Morrow 1999.

McCarthy, Cormac. *The Road.* Alfred A. Knopf 2006.

Milne, A A. *The House at Pooh Corner.* Farshore 2016.

Mitchell, Margaret. *Gone With The Wind.* Vintage Arrow 2020.

Nagel, Thomas. *What is it Like to be a Bat?* The Philosophical Review 1974

O Toole, John Kennedy. *A Confederacy of Dunces.* Grove Weidenfeld 1994.

Proulx, Annie. *Brokeback Mountain.* Scribner 2005.

Roberts, Adam. *On.* Gollancz 2002

Smith, Tom Rob. *Child 44.* Grand Central Publishing 2009.

Various. *@outstanding.screenplays* 2023.

ABOUT THE AUTHOR

Jan-Andrew Henderson (J.A. Henderson) is the author of 40 children's, teen, YA, adult and non-fiction books. Published in the UK, USA, Australia, Canada and Europe, he has been shortlisted for fifteen literary awards and is the winner of the Doncaster Book Prize, the Aurealis Award and the Royal Mail Award.

He runs the Green Light Literary Rescue Service offering professional editing and assessments for literary bodies and individuals.

www.janandrewhenderson.com
www.thegreenlightliteraryrescueservice.com

Ingram Content Group UK Ltd.
Milton Keynes UK
UKHW051034210723
425545UK00009B/44